ESSENTIALS *of*
MUSIC MANAGEMENT

Credits

Lead author: Adam Webb, with contributions from Paul Bonham, Anneliese Harmon, Annabella Coldrick, Manasvi Dethekar, Harry Hodgkin and Dennis Muirhead (mediation chapter) and a wide range of MMF members referenced in the book.

Graphics: Victoria Ford

Illustration: Chloe Bacon

Typesetting: Duncan Potter at Riverside Publishing Solutions

Editor: Annabella Coldrick

ABOUT THE MUSIC MANAGERS FORUM I themmf.net

MMF is the world's largest professional community of music managers in the world with over 1200 managers based in the UK with global businesses. Since our inception in 1992 we have worked to educate, inform and represent our members as well as offering a network through which managers can share experiences, opportunities and information.

We engage, advise and lobby and provide a professional voice for wider industry issues relevant to managers.

The MMF runs training programmes, courses and events designed to educate and inform artist managers as well as regular seminars, open meetings, roundtables, discounts, workshops, investment programmes and the Artist & Manager Awards.

To join and access many of the resources mentioned in this book visit www.themmf.net/signup

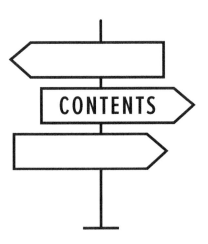

CONTENTS

PART 1: STARTING OUT

PART 2: GROWING YOUR MANAGEMENT BUSINESS

PART 3: SCALING UP & GOING GLOBAL

Chapter 10: Going Global

Chapter 11: Moving On. What Way To End It?

The Managers Backstage Toilet: Secrets, Tips

Preface

When the Music Managers Forum last published a "Bible" a decade ago the global music industry was in the throes of digital turmoil. This new book brings us up to date, and also takes account of how much the role of music management has changed in the intervening years.

As illustrated by the MMF's *Managing Expectations* report, over the past ten years, the trajectory of the music business and the combined impacts of technology, social media and sharing culture has led to more artist-centric models, and offered creators and music makers a far wider choice in how they take their music to market.

As a consequence of that shift, the role of the music manager has become far more pivotal, far more complex and far more demanding. In the words of MMF board member Ellie Giles, *"You're building a business for the artist. You're not actually a manager, you're a business developer."*

In addition to overseeing the core of their artists' recording and live work, managers are frequently taking responsibility in other areas such as PR and promotion, marketing, bookkeeping and accountancy. Managers are also increasingly acting as investors, and developing new types of partnerships with their clients. And they are likely to be juggling music management with a number of other jobs, especially in the early stages of their career.

For all these reasons, and because every manager's circumstances are different, we made a decision to present this book as a "guide" rather than a "bible". The MMF mantra is "there are no rules".

Despite this, management requires a broad knowledge of the whole music business across live, recorded, publishing, digital, physical, legal, brands and marketing to understand the current conventions and know why you are breaking them! We have aimed to cover all these areas, to make information as widely relevant as possible to managers of artists, songwriters, DJs *and* producers, and to incorporate expert comment and advice.

We wanted this book to reflect the journey of a manager's career: from the initial stages of developing an artist, through the process of scaling-up, bringing in expertise, building a team, growing a business and developing wider professional partnerships.

There are lots of other comprehensive books about the wider music industry, copyright and streaming including our very own Digital Dollar publications, we don't aim to replicate these great tomes but give a guide by managers for managers. We intend it to be an ever evolving digital compendium; like Kanye we will be regularly reviewing and updating so watch this space!

Annabella Coldrick, Chief Executive, MMF, 2022.

PART 1

Starting Out

CHAPTER 1

What is a Music Manager?

"Being a manager for me means taking responsibility and having initiative. It's our responsibility to bring together the creative talents and projects which meet the goals of the artist first and foremost and cultivate that for long term growth."

TK, Finesse Foreva

"Being a manager means being a part of moving an artist's vision forward in a way that really connects with people. The modes and direction can differ artist to artist and that keeps things fresh. As a music fan I have felt first hand the importance and value of that fan/artist connection and I believe there are endless possibilities for artists who understand the importance of that and have ideas of their own. I enjoy guiding that process."

Charlene Hegarty, Zero Myth Management

"Being a manager is a passion full of highs and lows – that comes with the job – no two days are the same EVER. You are in the driver's seat when it comes to dealing with campaigns & labels – so make sure you drive correctly!"

Kwame Kwaten – Vice Chairman MMF/ Ferocious Talent Management

"Being a manager is many things. Part advisor, part confidant. Part therapist, part listener. Part ambassador, part sounding board. At its very core, being a manager is protecting the ability for your clients to realise their creative potential. And fighting hard, anyone who seeks to diminish the value or importance of that. It's being a champion for the person, the music and the process."

Jill Hollywood, Echo Beach Management

WHO'S THE BOSS?

In one sense, the role of the music manager is pretty straightforward. The manager is hired by an artist, songwriter, composer, DJ, musician, producer, or other creative individual to oversee and enhance their music business.

There are many dynamics to an artist manager relationship. Managers work for the interests of the artist and their career, but it's not a traditional boss/employee situation. The manager-artist relationships are as individual and bespoke as can be, but the key thing to remember is that this is a partnership and should be based on mutual respect. The manager is there to provide strategic advice, creative input and help steer the business. However ultimately the artist must take responsibility for their own success (and failures!). The manager can be seen as the Chief Operating Officer of the business whereas the artist is the Chief Executive.

Unlike other parts of the music industry – such as recording, publishing or live – which operate mostly in their own silo, the manager takes a holistic approach both to their own business and the business of their client – helping develop, leverage and execute a strategy that delivers on the artist's goals.

As a result, managers need to be entrepreneurial. They must make things happen.

Meanwhile, the day-to-day workload of modern music management is becoming ever more complex.

The MMF's *Managing Expectations* report, published in 2019, highlights this shift in some detail – illustrating how managers now mostly see themselves as entrepreneurial business builders, overseeing all aspects of their clients career: from touring and ticketing, to accessing finance, registering works with collecting societies, overseeing recording contracts, developing marketing strategies, and liaising with streaming and social platforms, brands and A&R.

It's a demanding and sometimes all-encompassing workload. Although, as most managers will tell you, it can be fun too.

The job simultaneously straddles personal, creative and commercial boundaries – especially in the early stages of a manager's career, when resources are tight and you'll likely be juggling multiple roles.

There will be important administration and paperwork to take care of. Managers will oversee contracts, sign-off on campaigns, chase payments, plan and develop strategies and schedules, and ensure registrations are submitted.

This requires persistence and resilience. Managers are typically both strong-minded and good communicators. They're required to unlock new opportunities, understand developing trends and technologies, and build professional relationships that benefit their artists.

In addition to being a salesperson and cheerleader, a good manager is also a trusted confidante – providing creative guidance, and A&R skills, and acting as an initial sounding board for new music or ideas.

Alongside a fiduciary duty of care (i.e. ensuring your client's financial interests are treated as paramount), a manager might also invest financially or partner in their artist's business.

"The biggest challenge for managers now is working smart to ensure you have the right balance of income (so it's sustainable) but also having the time to be creative and entrepreneurial. You can't just do one thing anymore in my opinion – that applies to both managers and creatives. Managers definitely tend to wear way more hats these days and definitely can't get complacent."

Hannah Joseph, Decibelle

And, importantly, they will also play a protective role – ensuring their artist is provided creative space, and given the opportunity to work and develop their craft, as well as providing a degree of safeguarding for their well-being and mental health.

Just as no two artists are the same, no two music management businesses are either – and a manager's ambitions or business goals will typically be based around the creative or commercial objectives of their clients – for instance, to reach a certain number of streams, to collaborate with a specific producer, to perform at a certain venue or festival, to feature in a specific magazine, to make a certain type of recording.

Similarly, the manager's work schedule will depend, on the creative flow of the artist, songwriter or producer – and on the reaction of audiences to that creativity. A "hit" might take an artist around the world and open up thousands of opportunities; a "miss" might stall momentum, set things backwards or lead to doors being closed.

Ultimately, managers are facilitators – working to protect, develop and further their artist's long-term and short-term interests.

Music management is rapidly becoming a diverse and professionalised job. The MMF's membership has expanded dramatically over recent years, and has now surpassed 1,200, with significant increases in managers under 30, female managers and managers from Black, Asian and other ethnic backgrounds.

Perhaps most importantly, music management is open to everyone. This is not a profession based on qualifications but skills – it is dependent on characteristics, personality, taste and partnerships – underpinned by an ethical code of practice.

By its very nature, music management is difficult to categorise and put into a box, and the role has become increasingly idiosyncratic, personalised and tailored around the unique needs of the artists being represented. What works for a manager operating in electronic or hip hop, for instance, might not be feasible for a manager representing pop writers, or a heavy rock band or a producer.

All will structure their businesses in different ways, according to their client's strengths and weaknesses.

What we have tried to do is to map the trajectory of how a manager might build their business – from Part One, where we look at the fundamentals of setting up and developing an artist, to Part Two where we explore devolving responsibilities and building a team, to Part Three and taking that team global.

We can't promise to cover every aspect of management in depth, or in the order that a manager will experience their career; but we have tried to draw on expert views and opinions – even if those opinions occasionally conflict – and to link out to recommended sources of information. This book focuses mainly on growing an artist management business although we do also reference producer, songwriter and DJ management as these are all interlinked although not the same. For more detail on producer and songwriter management please read our 2021 publication 'Managing Expectations: the Producer and Songwriter edition' available for free on our website.

The beauty of digital publishing means we can update and amend future editions, as well as bring in fresh views and new thinking.

Music management never stays still. Which is why it's so exciting.

ROUTES TO MUSIC MANAGEMENT

Managers come from all walks of life. A common incoming enquiry at MMF is from talent asking us to find them a manager.

Although we do take down their details and make them available to our members, the majority of artist/manager relationships come together slightly more randomly.

The majority of the MMF's membership came into the profession via one of two routes – either from gaining experience inside the industry, or they're effectively self-taught and they came in from outside the music business.

In the former camp, many MMF members were initially working in an entirely different part of the music industry, or continue to combine management with other roles in music.

For instance, they might have been a journalist or worked at a record label or live agency, before stepping into management and utilising their existing expertise and connections. Similarly, there are also artists, songwriters and other music makers who make the move from creator to manager. MMF research suggests that around half of UK-based managers are in this position – either juggling the role with other employment, or taking on other supplementary work with the aspiration of becoming a manager full-time.

Routes to music management

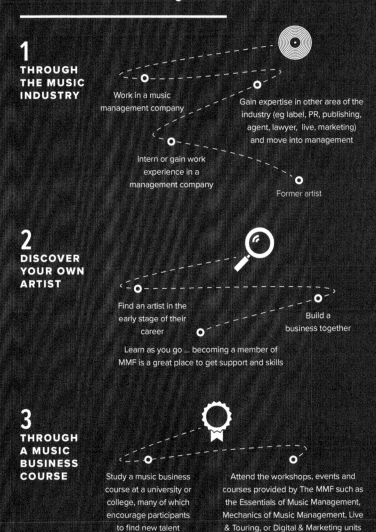

1 THROUGH THE MUSIC INDUSTRY

Work in a music management company

Gain expertise in other area of the industry (eg label, PR, publishing, agent, lawyer, live, marketing) and move into management

Intern or gain work experience in a management company

Former artist

2 DISCOVER YOUR OWN ARTIST

Find an artist in the early stage of their career

Build a business together

Learn as you go ... becoming a member of MMF is a great place to get support and skills

3 THROUGH A MUSIC BUSINESS COURSE

Study a music business course at a university or college, many of which encourage participants to find new talent

Attend the workshops, events and courses provided by The MMF such as the Essentials of Music Management, Mechanics of Music Management, Live & Touring, or Digital & Marketing units

There are also, of course, those who work at dedicated and established professional management companies, many starting in essential entry level positions around administristation and social media marketing.

In the latter camp are individuals who might be a friend, fan or relation of the artist – or even one of their parents – who started off helping out and eventually assumed responsibility for their business affairs. Many of the most successful music managers became established in this way.

You may identify with these descriptions, and these background circumstances will go some way to determining the professional relationship you enjoy with the artist you represent.

Ideally, and as detailed in the Code of Practice below, this relationship should be defined in a written agreement or contract. However, for those just starting out, it is more likely you will begin on a more ad hoc basis, with the relationship becoming formalised further down the line.

But whichever route you took, the one thing all good managers have in common is their desire to help and support artists.

"I found my first client through Instagram. What inspired me to take them one was they had a really cool hook that I helped develop into an actual song which ended up getting signed of Relentless Records."

Adrian Thomas, Rimes MGNT

"My management career grew out of my bedroom DIY cassette label Memorials of Distinction. Porridge Radio's early solo recordings were on my first compilation. I egged them on as a full band and helped record their debut album in a shed. When it became clear that other, more serious labels with real money and resources were interested, I decided to try to stay involved somehow, and I figured that meant 'managing' them."

Josh Cohen, Memorials of Distinction

One MMF member describes the job as a "vocation". It's a job with a mission that draws you back in — even if you think you want to get out!

ETHICS OF MUSIC MANAGEMENT & MMF CODE OF PRACTICE

The MMF's Code of Practice, which all members are required to sign up to and comply with, offers a comprehensive breakdown of the professional standards and duties expected of all managers.

1 Protect and promote the interests of their clients to the highest possible standard, devoting sufficient time so as to properly fulfil requirements and duties.

2 Be committed (and duty bound) to absolute transparency in all contractual and financial business dealings that concern their client;

3 Encourage having a written agreement in place between themselves and their client, recommending the artist seeks and receives independent legal advice before signing;

4 Before entering into a management relationship with an artist, make all reasonable efforts to confirm that the artist has fulfilled their legal obligations to the previous manager, if applicable and, if possible, assist them in doing so;

5 Not act in any fashion which is detrimental to their clients' interests and conduct themselves in a manner which is professional and ethical, and which abides by best business practices, complying with (and keeping abreast of) all relevant laws and legislation to the best of their ability; including legal frameworks that govern working with minors such as attaining DBS checks, and anti-discrimination laws such as the 2010 UK Equalities Act.

6 Not engage in any acts of sexual harassment including unwanted, unwelcome or uninvited behaviour of a sexual nature, which makes a person feel offended, humiliated or intimidated;

7 Make reasonable efforts to address any issues around mental health and wellbeing (including issues such as substance abuse) for both the artist they represent and themselves, signposting appropriate support resources where necessary;

8 Where a manager also acts independently for the client in any other capacity (publisher, label, agent, producer etc), they shall declare such interests and recommend their client receives independent expert advice to help them determine if there is a conflict of interest. The manager should not charge an artist multiple fees or commissions on the same revenue stream, even when acting in multiple capacities, unless there are exceptional circumstances which justify doing so. If such circumstances do apply, the manager should gain the written consent of the artist (following the artist's receipt of legal advice) before applying such additional fees or commissions;

9 Where the manager has control of some or all of the client's income, ensure that that income and expenditure is recorded and managed completely separately to the private assets of the manager. In addition, all transactions and records should be open for the inspection of the client or their appointed representative with reasonable notice.

10 Ensure that the managers share of the proceeds coming from their client's professional activity is commensurate to the level of investment the manager has provided, in time or financially.

The MMF has a complaints and dispute resolution process if it is believed a member does not comply with the provisions of the code which you can read on our website.

Recently and for good reason there has been an increased focus on the issues around bullying and harassment in the creative industries. Whilst #MeToo began with the film industry, music and television have both been under the spotlight as areas where the personal and professional blur to the detriment of those working in the sector. Power and influence come into play and the lack of formal HR processes in a sector mainly made up of freelancers. High profile cases involving artist, label executives, promoters and managers have increased the spotlight on these issues. It's important to remember that while managers and artists in many cases are friends, this is ultimately a professional relationship that comes with a duty of care. For example our sector has a long history of drug and alcohol use and whilst all adults are personally responsible for their own actions, a managers' role should be to help their clients seek and secure help should it be needed and be aware of risky situations which can be career ending for both parties. If working with artists who are minors or vulnerable, legal safeguarding measures come into play and any manager signing with a young artist should absolutely ensure they comply with the law such as DBS checks.

The UK Government in particular has been taking this very seriously and is exploring the creation of an Independent Standards Authority (ISA) where complaints can be taken by freelancers working in the creative industries. In the meantime the MMF is helping fund the development of training modules which will be available to managers with guidance and directing both managers and artists to Help Musicians helpline on Bullying and Harassment on 0845 22 55 787 which offers anyone working within the music industry:

- A confidential space to share your experience
- Support to resolve your situation
- Guidance and information on your options

Managers should be aware that evidence of non-compliance with the principles of the code (which follow UK law) can be used as a reason to terminate a management contract, so we would encourage all new and existing managers to ensure you are familiar with the key provisions and contact the MMF should you need any additional support or advice on any of these issues.

SECURING FINANCE

For all managers, whether just starting out or overseeing the career of a global megastar, a fundamental part of their remit is finance. This is to raise revenue for the artist they work with, to keep the money coming in, to ensure that any revenues are being managed efficiently and to explore new potential sources of income.

All artists – and indeed managers – require money and investment to reach their creative and commercial goals.

It is a manager's responsibility to find that finance, and in a way that balances an artist's short-term necessities with their long-term aspirations. That means evaluating and agreeing the right kinds of partnerships for your client, not simply those that pay the most or result in the greatest commission.

Crucially, they need to serve the interests of the artist, while also ensuring that their own business remains viable.

HOW DO MANAGERS GET PAID?

Investing in new talent development can take many years to pay off. Whether you are working with artists, producers or songwriters, honing a craft, and building a market it is rarely an instantaneous endeavour. This means that in the early days the manager is investing as much as their client, often working unpaid for years in order to build their clients career to the point where they can both earn. As a consequence many managers have mixed business models whether they work other jobs during this period, or manage a range of clients (producers, writers, artists) or their client base combines new and very established talent so they can make ends meet until it takes off.

MUSIC CLIENT & MANAGER AGREEMENTS

Historically, most managers have worked to a commission-based model – providing a defined set of services and *typically* accruing 20% of their artist's gross income once certain pre-agreed expenses are deducted. This can however be higher or lower depending on the experience of the manager/artist and the range of services they provide.

This means that the manager earns only when their client earns – which is obviously fine if the music creator is making decent revenue, but hugely challenging when they are in development and requiring investment!

These arrangements are also frequently confined to a certain time scale or period of activity, ensuring that the manager can only commission against a specific set of activities – e.g. for recordings that were released under the period of the management contract.

According to MMF research, two-thirds of managers still operate their business around commission-based earnings. For these individuals, it is therefore imperative to have complete clarity both on the percentage of commission charged, and on which activities will be commissionable.

How do managers get paid?

"20% COMMISSION" RULES

66%

Despite a diversification of the music business, 66% of respondents still rely on commission-based earnings. 75% of these are on a 20% commission.

PAY DISPARITY

25%

earn more than the national average. But 56% earn less than £10k per annum from music management. 21% earn nothing at all.

LIVE

IS NOW THE MOST SIGNIFICANT REVENUE STREAM

Followed by recorded/ publishing advances, PRS royalties, streaming payments and PPL royalties

DIFFERENT MODELS IN MANAGEMENT

While 52% of respondents are full-time employees, or run their own company full-time, the remainder represent a wide cross-section of part-time, freelance and contractual workers

---

FULL-TIME VS. PART-TIME

52%   48%

Full-time employees   Part-time, etc.

BUT NO US VS. THEM

26%

work full-time or part-time in another part of the music business

---

NOT ENOUGH HOURS IN THE DAY...

Hours dedicated to music management

25%
less than 19 hours per week

40%
more than 40 hours

23%
more than 49 hours

er, commissions won't work for everyone, and among the MMF's membership
seeing managers adopt a diversifying range of commercial agreements
ir artists – including monthly retainers, joint ventures and partnerships (for
e, starting a record label together), or managers offering a combination of
vices based on a commission alongside additional paid-for consultancy or
services.

Meanwhile, managers working in established management companies will typically
receive a salary, which might then be supplemented by a cut of commission or a
bonus.

The MMF's **Managing Expectations** report highlights a number of these alternative
models.

However, whichever models you end up opting for your business, and as reiterated in the MMF's Code of Practice, it is vital to establish the boundaries of your commercial relationship at the earliest possible opportunity – ensuring from the get-go that you're committed to being fully open and transparent in all your business dealings.

In other words, right from the start, you should communicate with your clients about how your partnership will work commercially, how finances will be split and the workload you will be expected to undertake.

One thing we try to encourage at the MMF is for managers to understand and appreciate the viability of their own business – as well as those of their artist – and to ensure their own finances are sustainable. For example, it might be tempting to invest a certain sum of money in an artist in the earliest stage of their development – but if that is coming directly from the manager's back pocket, then it could potentially undermine their own long-term business strategy.

Certainly, if you are investing your own finances in a specific project (for instance, in a video or a recording session) then you should also be discussing how your investment will be compensated and have this subject to separate legal agreement.

A smart manager will often look for and exhaust potential sources of investment before spending their own money, or at the very least ensure that boundaries and structures are established at the earliest possible opportunity.

Importantly, the Code of Practice stresses, before entering into a binding commercial relationship, that an artist should receive independent legal advice, and that a

"As a manager, especially of an upcoming act, it can be really tempting to invest your own money in their career at too early a stage. In my work in Accelerator I encourage managers to consistently think about their own business needs first. If your business isn't sustainable, then the artists might not be in the long run. So many managers are happy to spend £500 or so in one area early without considering if they for example have formalised a relationship with a client or tested interest from the partners they hope to work with to see if the artist is viable in the market."

Paul Bonham, Professional Development Director, MMF

manager should make all reasonable efforts to confirm that, if applicable, the artist has fulfilled their legal obligations to any previous manager.

Basing your partnership on such strong and clear foundations is essential – albeit, in the early developmental stage of an artist's career, financial outgoings and investment will likely exceed an artist's incoming revenues.

Formalising your relationship

For this reason, the MMF advocates considering a trial period or short-form "letter of engagement" (e.g. for a defined 6 month period) before any binding legal agreement is reached. MMF members can download a template for a six month "letter of engagement" to help instruct this process.

Indeed, every manager we've spoken to when researching this book has repeated the same piece of advice: before entering into a formal contract, always test the waters with a clearly-defined trial period. This should detail specifically what revenues you would be commissioning on.

As one manager put it to us, always do six months together on a temporary basis – if you're not together after that, then there's literally no point in carrying on.

Other managers have recommended trial periods of up to a year, while some will work to even longer schedules before formalising a relationship.

The MMF's Code of Practice makes clear that, at the very least, managers should *"encourage having a written agreement in place between themselves and their client"* and that the client should *"seek and receive independent legal advice before signing"*.

Moreover, the Code of Practice also recommends that a manager should also *"make all reasonable efforts to confirm that the artist has fulfilled their legal obligations to any previous manager, if applicable, and, if possible, assist them in doing so."*

That said, some managers have claimed they find contracts can be inflexible.

For others, regardless of any pre-written agreement, the most crucial commodity of their relationship is "trust".

Whatever your circumstances and outlook, good communications are absolutely imperative – and even for someone completely new to music management, you should at least aim to establish boundaries and clearly outline the specific tasks you will be undertaking for your artist.

"Someone told me when I first became a manager that the manager/client relationship should always be strictly business, not friendship, because when feelings get involved things get messy. I've done the complete opposite of that, management is so much more rewarding when it feels like family because you're always going to work harder for people you love. Telling a band who are like family to you, that they'd been nominated for a huge award is a pretty incredible feeling."

Louise Latimer, East City Management

For many upcoming managers, that workload will probably encompass a bit of everything; a key first objective for managers is developing the investment and capacity for the wider team around the client. As managers build partnerships for their artists with agents, labels, distributors or publishers, and brands and the cash begins to flow; then formalising your business partnership makes a lot of sense. For more information on management contracts see Part Two of this book.

BANK ACCOUNTS & BUSINESS STRUCTURES

One immediate consideration for both yourself and your artist is you think about business structures and bank accounts.

While it is important that your management business and your client's business are separated – so they can receive revenues directly – it will also be practical for you to be a countersignature to their account to ensure the smooth running of their business.

So while there should be a clear and distinct separation between your two commercial operations (and, in fact, you will be invoicing that business) in practice you will also need oversight of their account in order to help grow their career.

Aside from the obvious practicalities of opening a bank account to keep incoming and outgoing finances in one centralised place, it should also help determine the structure of their business – for instance, if it's a band with multiple members, do they all have an equal stake? Do they share equally in songwriting and recording revenues?

Also, importantly, who is responsible for invoicing, payments and filing accounts?

And are these functions where they would like assistance to oversee and help with administration from professional accountants, business managers or bookkeepers?

Once your client starts receiving income then a business is automatically formed – which means it makes sense for that income to go into a separate bank account, accessible and accountable to all relevant parties.

Many of these same considerations will also apply to your own management business and how it is structured. Even if you or your client take no active steps to establish a business, you will be considered a Sole Trader. Similarly, if you or your client operate as a group, collective or band, and if all members have an equal stake in the business, then, by default, it will become a Partnership. This simplicity does offer some advantages. For instance, you can carry on using your own bank account.

However, Sole Trader or Partnership status means that you or your artists are personally responsible for your business – including any debts incurred. You would also be expected to register with HMRC and file an annual self-assessment tax return. This is particularly worth flagging for Partnerships, as all members share liabilities – even if only one member is responsible for creating them.

So simplicities do come with risks attached. Being personally liable for debts means that if your business hits rocky times or if you face legal actions, then your savings or property could potentially be seized.

For this reason, most semi-mature businesses with any degree of complexity eventually set up as a **Private Limited Company (PLC)** or **Limited Liability Company (LLC)**.

In effect, both structures establish a separate legal entity, and limit the personal exposure of directors or shareholders if finances take a downward turn. It is the company that enters into contracts with third parties, not individuals – albeit both PLCs and LLCc come with additional reporting and administrative requirements, often undertaken by an accountant at additional cost.

As a PLC or LLC, you would typically become a director and shareholder of the new venture, offering you far greater protections and flexibility to grow your business. Additionally, running a PLC or LLC is generally considered more tax efficient than operating as a Sole Trader or Partnership.

However, setting up a PLC or LLC means that certain information about the company, including profits and losses and contact details, are made publicly available at Companies House. Therefore, the company does not have the privacy afforded to a Sole Trader or Partnership.

In practice, some managers and artists will operate as both Sole Traders/ Partnerships *and* PLCs/LLCs. For instance, if an artist is signed to a label or publisher, it might be more efficient to receive revenues from recordings or songwriting through a Sole Trader business. However, when it comes to live touring, which holds a lot more risks, having a limited company might be more advantageous.

Whichever route you choose, you would be advised to contact HMRC as soon as possible.

For example, if you want to be a Sole Trader, then you'll need to register as Self Employed in order to pay a tax return. You might also consider employing the services of an accountant, who can offer advice on business administration and expenses, as well as taking on the responsibility of submitting paperwork to HMRC.

If you are in business with a partner, or your clients are members of a group, then it would also be prudent to formulate a written agreement to define the parameters of ownership – for instance, how will bills be paid, how will revenue be allocated, how will financial decisions be made, and what happens in the eventuality that a band member or partner decides to leave.

Obviously some of these technicalities will be easier to address if you or your client operate solo. For more information about setting up a business we advise you go to https://www.gov.uk/set-up-business

Unless entering into a joint venture together, it is imperative that there is a clear separation between the businesses of the manager and the business of the client.

Revenues should flow into the client-controlled bank account, and as a manager you will most likely be invoicing the artist for your payment or commission.

We will explore the mechanics of how the management and artist businesses interact, and the role of accountants, in part two.

ACCOUNTANT TIPS: ELLA LUBY, GENERAL MANAGER MSE BUSINESS MANAGEMENT LLP

Register for Taxes

You are obliged to file a tax return when you start earning any income outside of a payroll. A simple self-assessment registration can be completed online with HMRC without professional advice.Even if you're making losses – these are important to be able to offset against future profits.

Bank Accounts

Maintain separate bank accounts for your:

- personal finances,
- management business and
- client monies

It is important to maintain clarity and transparency (especially when dealing with money on behalf of artists) between your different financials, and your accountant will be endlessly grateful!

Invoicing & Income

Keep invoice numbers sequential – don't change per artist or client. For example 2022/001, 2022/002.

Invoice all your management commissions, even if you don't expect them to be paid – it will demonstrate how much you are investing in your clients.

Review income by artist and type of income e.g. royalties, live, merch, etc. – it will give you a solid understanding of which clients you are earning from (also who you're not) and where they are earning income. This will help you to make future decisions about their businesses, and help you earn your commissions.

Royalty Statements

Firstly, open them. Spend time understanding them.

Know who they come from, when and how to get payments owed.

Make sure you understand them to know when to ask the right questions. If you don't know what questions to ask, ask that question from other managers, your accountant or the company sharing the report with you.

Find An Entertainment Accountant
Even if you and your clients are not quite ready, get to know what options there are and build an idea of who you would like to work with. The MMF has a list of associates who are happy to help.

Some accountants are happy to provide free advice to ensure you are set up correctly from the off. Starting on the right foot early can avoid a lot of work later down the line.

As soon as income starts to gain momentum, and certainly when you have an artist deal in the pipeline, seek advice – there are some clever tools accountants can use to plan ahead, and help you keep more of your money, but we can only do it before the deal, not after.

What Makes a Good Artist/Manager Relationship?
Aside from a genuine belief and passion for creative talent, most managers will look for other specific stand-out attributes before committing to work with a new artist or producer – whether that's a degree of passion, drive, work ethic and ambition, or simply what they view as untapped commercial potential.

"Trust is essential in any manager relationship. Trust in your manager to enhance your career with solid, truthful advice and trust from the manager in what the artist is creating. Of course, there will be some hurdles along the way, but staying true to a united vision with the manager tirelessly working as the captain of that ship is also essential."

Stephen "Tav" Taverner, East City Management

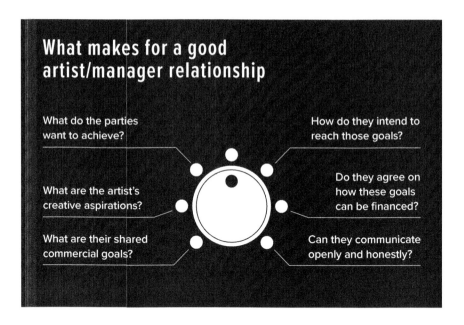

What makes for a good artist/manager relationship

What do the parties want to achieve?

How do they intend to reach those goals?

What are the artist's creative aspirations?

Do they agree on how these goals can be financed?

What are their shared commercial goals?

Can they communicate openly and honestly?

Attributes Managers Look for in Artists

- Their strengths and weaknesses
- The genres they fit into
- Their potential audience demographic
- Their potential champions in media and the industry
- Their core values
- Other similar artists or potential creative collaborators they can work with
- Their unique selling point and skills in a competitive market

Typically, this connection will also manifest itself into an initial conversation of how you intend to work together:

- What does the client want to achieve?
- What are their creative aspirations?
- What are their commercial goals?
- How do they intend to reach those goals?
- And how is this going to be financed?

While some creatives do manage themselves, for the vast majority, as they start to build an audience and regular work; the demands of business will eventually detract and distract from their creative endeavours.

All creatives need finance to continue making music; and as they scale-up and gain momentum, the services of a manager can help unlock the additional investment and opportunities that support their business, as well as provide them with structure and organisation.

Early into a relationship most managers will look to brainstorm with their client to establish a short-to-medium-term plan that will provide a basic trajectory, for instance:

- A list of goals — eg to perform at a certain venue, festival or platform, to collaborate with a certain producer, artist or brand, to be reviewed by a certain publication, achieve a number of cuts, or reach a number streams
- A business plan — how are you going to finance the next 12 months ahead?

Examples of short-term goals might include writing a bio, arranging a photoshoot, establishing social channels, finding other producers, songwriters and artists, or organising a regular rehearsal space.

Longer-term goals, which might be dependent on external factors or stepping stones, might include touring around the UK, signing to a particular record label or publisher, or striking a certain brand deal.

Once provided with this information, it's the manager's job to establish a viable commercial strategy ahead — and to incorporate this into their own business plan.

For this partnership to be viable in the long term, it is hugely important that an artist's goals align with their manager's ambitions, skills, capacity and long term objectives.

DEVELOPING YOUR MANAGEMENT BUSINESS

As well as developing your client's business and helping set their goals and aspirations, it is also hugely important that you can formulate a strategy around your own management business. In the cut and thrust of the music business, this is easy to lose sight of!

Good questions to ask yourself might be:

- Which managers do you look up to as inspiration?
- Do you want to manage multiple artists or music creators?

- What aspirations do you have for your own business? Do you have a business plan in place?
- What do you see as your personal strengths and areas where you'd like to gain experience or outside expertise?
- What metrics of success do you want for your artists? Commercial "hits"? International reach? Both or something else?
- Do you need to find artists that will attract upfront investment? Or are you looking to hold on to rights ownership in the long run?
- Will management create a conflict alongside any of your pre-existing business interests – for instance, if you do or want to run a label or publishing company?
- Do you need any additional support in these initial steps? For instance, from an investor or mentor?
- At what point will you need additional business support from a lawyer or an accountant?

THE ECONOMICS OF ARTISTS, SONGWRITERS, PRODUCERS AND DJS

In order to make a success of music management it is essential you have an understanding of the different revenue streams available to music creators, how those revenue streams can feed into one another and – based on their business plan – which will be the greatest priority for you and your client.

They can be very different for artists (some earning 80% from live), songwriters (mostly from publishing/CMOs), producers (session fees and royalties) and DJs (live performance fees).

Fundamentally, these revenues will provide the basis for both of your businesses.

Historically, there have been four core ways for creatives to make money: recording and songwriting, live performance, and direct-to-fan (ie everything else, including merchandise and brand partnerships).

Recording and Songwriting
This part of an artist's business is based around their creation of intellectual property. Every recording inherently contains two separate copyrights: one for the underlying song, and one for the recording. For more detail on how copyright works read the MMF's Dissecting the Digital Dollar books or many of the excellent music industry books including Ann Harrison's 'Music the Business' now on its 8th edition.

How an artist makes money

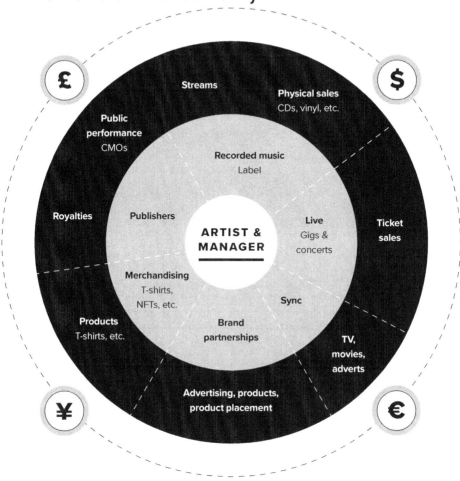

Consequently, whenever a track is played on a streaming service, broadcast on the radio, or sold as a CD or vinyl purchase, it triggers two separate payments.

1 The Master or Performance Right.
The master income is generated from sales or streams of recorded music – for instance, when a CD album is purchased in a shop, or when a track is consumed on a service like Spotify or YouTube. Artists, producers, performers and labels

also receive royalties when their recordings are broadcast on the radio or TV. In the UK, this revenue is collected and administered by PPL – making it hugely important that you register your performers and their recordings as soon as they are made publicly available. At the time of writing, joining PPL is free and can be done online.

Typically, the master right is owned by whoever paid for a recording. We will explore the different kinds of services and deal types in a later chapter.

In addition to PPL for the master rights, it is advised that you register your writer's works with PRS and MCPS (or another collecting society) as soon as their work is made publicly available.

2   The Publishing or Song Rights.

These are owned by the writers of the recording – who control the invisible "intellectual property" of the composition, including its composition and lyrics. In practice, this could mean ownership by a single writer, or it might stretch to any combination of composers, producers, or musicians – including samples of other recordings.

From here, song rights can be broken down three ways: "performance rights" (where the composer receives royalties whenever a song is broadcast or performed), "mechanical rights" (where the composer receives royalties whenever a song is reproduced or sold, for instance when a record is purchased) and "synchronisation rights" (where a song is placed into a film, TV show, advert or other visual medium).

Many composers will sign a deal with a publisher or a publishing administration company to manage their song rights, which means the publisher also receives a percentage of their royalties for the services they provide.

The vast majority of songwriters will also register with a collecting society (in the UK, this is PRS) and mandate them to collect their performance royalties on a global basis. They will also register works with a collecting society for mechanical royalties (in the UK, this is MCPS, which operates under a service agreement with PRS).

At the time of writing, it costs £100 each to join PRS and MCPS as a one-off fee.

A more detailed explanation of these revenue streams can be found in the MMF's *Dissecting The Digital Dollar.*

3 Live Music & Performance.

The bulk of live revenue is generated through the sales of tickets to performances at gigs, concerts and festivals. Songwriters also receive revenue from live shows or DJ sets through a levy on ticket sales (4.2% in the UK), ensuring they are paid for any performances of their work. Another good reason to register with a collecting society!

4 Direct-to-Fan & Partnership Revenues.

These account for everything else, including merchandise sales, commercial brand partnerships, and other direct-to-fan commerce or new technologies. There is more detail on these income streams later in the chapter.

Before going any deeper, a good exercise at this point would be to develop a simple cash flow and business plan tailored around the expected incomes you will think you will generate from your artists.

"Working with brands from an early stage can really help build the story for your artist. I use this as an additional tool when it comes to the music travelling and building character within a campaign. Brands have helped us reach audiences from London to Sydney and I often find that fashion translates just as fast and just as clearly as the music does."

Cillian Farrell, Kill Management

"For me it's really important having a plan for myself, to look back on and see am I in terms of progression, am I where I needed to be financially, is my artist on the trajectory we had planned together."

Jess Slater, Munroe Management

"How you define success is so important. Building a plan that's adaptable but ambitious is the key. A great source of unhappiness is feeling you're a failure – if it didn't work out get another artist, get another deal. You will be unhappy forever if you don't realise what your true purpose is, which in most cases isn't for one artist – there will be a thousand failures if you look around, and that's okay. That meant they tried and learned from it."

Anneliese Harmon Music Exec, Entrepreneur and GM at MMF

By doing this, you can start to build realistic goals and milestones for both yourself and your artist.

How To Approach Business Planning.

In addition to these "traditional" revenue streams, brand opportunities and increasingly rapid technological change continues to open new revenue-generating and investment-raising opportunities to artists and their managers – for instance, with NFTs and the creation of other digital assets, or with new variations of crowdfunding and direct-to-fan interaction.

Not all of these will be appropriate or applicable for all artists, but, for the savvy entrepreneur, the doors are wide open to pursue alternative sources of revenue that probably wouldn't even have existed only a few years ago.

CHAPTER 2

Creative Development

Management isn't only about commercial skills, it is also about helping your artist reach their creative and artistic potential. Without great songwriting and composition, and without great music and performances, your job as a manager will be redundant. You can have the greatest marketing or promotional plans in the world, but if it's not backed up by music that excites and entertains an audience, then it's all likely to fall flat.

For this reason, artist development (sometimes called A&R – an abbreviation of "artists and repertoire") is one of the most crucial skill sets a manager can acquire. According to MMF research, our members are increasingly taking charge of the development process, and often before a label or other partner gets involved.

Broadly speaking, this developmental work falls into two categories:

THE PRACTICAL

Administrating – registering titles, works and compositions with PROs

Booking rehearsal rooms or studio space – providing an artist the opportunity to practice or make demos

Collaborating – networking with other managers or industry professionals to build creative relationships – e.g. with other artists, producers, songwriters, mixers, engineers or musicians.

Curating – overseeing which tracks and images are made public, and helping to shape your artist's identity and story

Development and coaching – developing your artists musicianship, performance and craft by opening opportunities such as tuition, workshops or songwriting camps

Equipping – most creators will require a basic understanding of music production software (eg Logic, Pro Tools, Ableton), as well as instruments, microphones and amplifiers

Financing – accessing enough money to underwrite your artist's plans

Organising – locating performing opportunities such as shows or showcases, getting your artist booked and performing in front of the most appropriate audience, taking care of logistics (eg. transport) and ensuring payment is received

Promoting – sending recordings to press, radio, influencers and tastemakers and championing your artist to others in the industry

THE PERSONAL

Direction – helping select key tracks for demos, decide setlist, advice on videos, content, image and presentation

Feedback – offering personal views and opinions on new material and performance

Preparation – helping decide when your artist is market / stage / platform ready

Support – dealing with setbacks, problem solving and providing solutions

Vicky Dowdall, CEO, VDM Music

IN YOUR EXPERIENCE, HOW HANDS ON IS THE MANAGER'S ROLE IN CREATIVE DEVELOPMENT OR A&R?

"At the start managers have to wear lots of hats as you don't have a team in place, no record deal, no publisher, and I have been very involved with the A&R. I would identify who would be a good collaborator for the artist so they can develop their sound together. I get involved in giving feedback on the songs, the production and the mix and help decide what songs we are going to release along with the artist. Cody Frost for example is a massive Enter Shikari fan so it made sense to put her with Dan Weller (Shikari 's producer). For Nina Nesbitt we don't have an A&R so we make all of the creative decisions together."

David Prince Yeboah, GS Entertainment Management

"The early stage of development involves seeking out the talent for commercial development. I oversee the recording process and align my client with the right producers in order to create the right sound. I work closely with the artist, acting as their liaison with the producers and writers and as an advisor who will help nurture their unique sound and image. I have creative input but only in the form of guidance, I let the artist fully express themselves."

Ultimately, most managers would want to see themselves in the role of "critical friend" and capable of offering objective and truthful feedback to their artist.

RECORDING & DIY RELEASING

Before you start thinking about record or publishing deals, your artist will probably need to start composing some music and making it available – either as high quality demos that you can circulate to potential industry partners, or suitable tracks for public consumption.

These might be privately uploaded to DropBox, or publicly available on a user-generated content (UGC) platform such as SoundCloud, TikTok or YouTube, or a

Digital Service Platform (DSP) such as Spotify, Apple Music, YouTube Music, Deezer or TIDAL.

In all likelihood, the artist, songwriter or producer you're working with will already be testing the waters here – and certainly with the UGC services. These days, the majority of artists start their creative journey by posting original tracks, collaborations or cover versions online; and this is where many managers and industry professionals start to scout for talent.

However, when a manager comes onboard, there's likely to be a more strategic discussion about what kind of tracks are posted, where they are posted, and how they are promoted. That's likely to be coupled with a conversation about identity or branding, and ensuring the artist is uploading good quality photos and a basic biography – including contact details, and social media accounts – that projects an appropriate image.

Although some managers are quite relaxed about an artist continuing to post music and content online, others will advise removing all pre-existing audio and video content – effectively giving their client a chance to retrench, wipe the slate clean, and re-establish themselves.

Ultimately, these decisions are down to the artist.

However, other considerations for a manager at this early stage might be:

- What are your artists initial goals?
- Which audience are you targeting?
- From which services or stores does your audience consume music?
- What else is going on in your segment of the market?
- What is your artist's brand identity?
- Is now the time to start sending music to potential supporters and tastemakers?

DIY Releasing
Although some UGC sites do offer the facility for users to make money (for instance, YouTube operates a Partner Programme allowing artists to take a share of advertising revenue) it is the major streaming services and download stores, as well as physical sales of vinyl and CDs, that offer the best opportunity to drive revenues from recorded music.

Obviously, for the majority of artists, their initial releases do not necessarily generate huge sales or streams. At the time of writing, tens of thousands of tracks are ingested into streaming services every day, and there is competition everywhere – not just in music – for attention. Rising above the noise and standing out is incredibly challenging.

On the positive side, the barriers to entry and releasing music have never been lower or more affordable.

So it clearly makes sense to think outside the box, and to develop a release plan with your artist that determines how they might build attention – whether that's through audio or video streaming services, through social media, through support from a local record shop or gig venue, through live shows, or via some other means.

Meanwhile, outside of the streaming platforms, specialist DIY music services, such as Bandcamp – which blends paid-for downloads with streaming and physical sales – have become pivotal to many artist's businesses; as are specialist download stores for certain dance or electronic genres (eg Beatport, Traxsource or Bleep).

Uploading music to these platforms is not a particularly onerous process, but, even as a self-releasing artist, there are multiple routes to market – all with implications for your artist's business.

However, before your client thinks about releasing their music commercially or making it publicly available, it is important that the ownership of that music is agreed, correctly apportioned and accurately uploaded. If this doesn't happen – and it's often the manager's job to make sure it is! – then it'll create a world of problems later down the line.

AGREEMENTS & SPLITS

A truly independent artist who has self-financed their own recordings will control 100% of their master rights. However, in many cases there will have been other people involved in the recording process – for instance, songwriters, producers, session musicians and engineers.

For that reason, if your artist paid for a recording then they should have agreements in place – ideally written agreements – with any contributors. This agreement should make a clear declaration about who owns the master rights, as well as conferring their contributions into that ownership.

On this basis, contributors can then negotiate a share of the master revenues – or what's commonly referred to as a "split".

For instance, if your artist employs the services of a producer, then the producer's agreement will typically assign all master rights (as above) in return for an upfront fee and a royalty – which might typically be between 2% and 5% or a similar pro rata of the artists royalty.

The agreement would then be date stamped to clarify when the terms become active – for instance, a producer royalty might only become active after certain costs, such as an advance, are recouped.

If your client is the producer, then you'd be on the other side of the fence in this negotiation of course, and attempting to agree an appropriate fee and royalty rate.

Alternatively, the producer might be paying for the studio time and the recording costs – in which case they would become the de facto owner of the master rights. Read more about the role of the producer and producer and writer managers in the MMF's Managing Expectations: Producer & Writer Edition.

Another increasingly common occurrence is when a manager invests in an artist's recording, and therefore technically takes ownership or part-ownership of the master. Under this scenario, it is important to clarify the implications of any investment, and how it impacts on any pre-arranged agreements on commissions.

But, however the splits are sliced and diced, they will need to be set in stone and agreed in advance.

If this does not happen then it increases the likelihood of royalties being unmatched or unallocated when a track is made available to stream or purchase, as well as disputes or even legal action.

The process of determining ownership of songwriting credits and split is also vitally important, and it is frequently the manager's responsibility to establish and pre-agree who contributed what to a composition.

For instance, a four-piece band might want to split songwriting four ways. Alternatively, if they have a single songwriter, then that individual might want to claim 100% of publishing royalties.

In another scenario, a dance artist might work with a team of songwriters and a producer, all of whom have a stake in the songwriting process.

To help with this process, the Musicians Union have some invaluable template forms – on Recording Agreements and Song Share Agreements on their website.

Alternatively, there are a number of apps available that allow splits to be agreed and designated, for instance, the Session app that aims to "capture authoritative creator data at the point of creation", or the Splits app developed by Creative Media Group.

In practice, these conversations will also require a human touch. Negotiation is an important skill and characteristic for managers to work on; developing their personal style and skills.

REGISTRATIONS – SONG & RECORDING MANAGEMENT

Once your agreements and splits are confirmed, it is crucial that these details are registered with your Performing Rights Organisation (PRO) – both for publishing / songwriter royalties, and for public performance of the master recordings.

Fail to do this and your clients will lose revenue if their track is broadcast or performed!

Remember, PRS and PPL collect revenue wherever music is played in public in a commercial setting (whether that's in a shop, a workplace, or a radio station or streaming service). MCPS collects songwriter/publisher royalties whenever a composition is "reproduced" (e.g. via a CD or vinyl sale, or a stream), while PRS also collects a levy on ticket sales in order to pay songwriters / publishers from live performances of their songs.

UK collecting societies have reciprocal partnerships with their overseas equivalents – meaning that if your client's music is broadcast or performed in another country, then they should still receive payment for the use of their work.

Unless you have a publisher assigned to take care of these tasks, it is typically a manager's responsibility to ensure that registrations are completed accurately and ahead of release. Managers will still need to oversee and ensure publishers have correct information throughout the assignment period ensuring catalogue and new titles are registered correctly and consistently.

Once your client has joined a collection society, the process to register works is straightforward and both UK services have client management services which should be able to help should you have difficulties, both PPL and PRS/MCPS have detailed information on their websites.

James Dawson, Jax Management

"PRS and PPL are probably the most regular and dependable revenue streams for every type of music creator. It's always worth double checking your song registrations are correct and making sure you're getting paid every penny you're owed. Whilst it can take a bit of effort to get the hang of the databases it certainly pays off long term and is an essential management skill to master"

Paul Bonham, MMF Professional Development Director

"Quite a few early stage managers I meet don't give enough attention to the importance of song royalties and registrations. It's by far the most long term and reliable income generation stream. Often managers feel if it's "the songwriter's money" they shouldn't commission. I ask them to consider their role in securing radio plays by chasing the promotions team or speaking directly to DJs? Who is facilitating the touring and engaging the shows? Engagement in these commissions early establishes a good working relationship, sustaining the manager to build a business. Managers are able to get third party mandates signed for both PRS and PPL so they can keep an eye on metadata, match songs to missing claims, and upload setlists, radio plays and tour dates."

UPLOADING MUSIC TO STREAMING SERVICES

Given the sheer volume of self released music uploaded to audio and video streaming services, most artists and managers will use an intermediary to encode and distribute their music – just as they would for physical products like CDs, vinyl or merchandise. This works best for the streaming services too, who would prefer to work with a handful of suppliers, rather than strike thousands of deals with individual artists.

Many of these intermediary distributors will help market and promote your artist's music, and find placements that might expand their audience.

Importantly, they will also be able to generate International Standard Recording Codes (or ISRCs) used for any released music embedded during mastering.They are unique digital fingerprints essential for downloadable and streamable tracks, and tracking radio play embedding them with ownership details (or metadata).

As with any other registrations, it is vital that ISRC information is correct, clear and coherent – including the spellings of track titles and the names of contributors. Get it wrong, and you risk your client not getting paid!

The different kinds of release partners and what they offer are explained in far greater detail in the MMF's Dissecting The Digital Dollar – and specifically in our Digital Deals Guide – but they will include:

Record labels:

A label deal effectively advances finance to the artist – supporting their recording career and livelihood, while also providing a range of manufacturing, promotional, distribution and marketing services.

In effect, the label will pay for records to be produced, and then ensure they are placed in stores and digital services. In exchange, they will agree a royalty rate for sales and streams – which is used to pay back the artist's "advance" (i.e. up-front signing on fee) and other recoupable costs. Historically, label deals confer ownership to the label, making them the de facto "owner" of the master rights for an agreed period of time.

The biggest major and indie labels will have direct relationships with all the big streaming services, while smaller labels or established independent artists and management companies will use third party distributors in order to upload their artists' music such as Republic of Music, PIAS or Cargo.

We go into more detail about record labels and the manager's role in deal negotiations also involving artist lawyers in Part Two.

Label Service Companies

The big difference between these companies and traditional record labels is that they look to "licence" masters from the artist for an agreed short-term period, rather than own those rights outright. However, there is a trade off. Label service companies tend to pay smaller advances focused around direct marketing costs, and will also occasionally demand additional costs for certain marketing or promotional work.

Consequently, these licensing deals can result in the manager having to assume a greater share of workload and responsibility acting as a pseudo "label manager". Having been pioneered by companies like Absolute, AWAL, Believe and Tunecore, all three major labels also now offer "service" deals too through their ownership of companies such as Virgin Music Artist & Label Services (Universal Music), Spinnup (Universal Music), The Orchard (Sony) and ADA (Warner Music). More about negotiating label services deals can be found in Part Two.

DIY Distributors

There are also a range of specialist distribution companies who typically offer a flat fee for an artist to upload and distribute music to multiple streaming platforms and record stores. These services will often offer a range of bolt-on services, including data analytics tools, and a range of marketing and promotional services – for instance playlist pitching, calculation of royalty splits, PR or social media support.

In return for a one-off fee, they allow the artist to retain total ownership of their work and collect 100% of revenue generated. Some of the most well-known DIY services include:

Amuse: Offer a range of service packages, including a free tier, and also an advance royalties payment service.

CD Baby: US-based business, operating a pay-per-release model. CD Baby also offers a music publishing package and can manufacture and distribute CDs.

Distrokid: Offer a single all-in subscription for unlimited releases.

Ditto: Founded in the UK, Ditto offers a range of packages for releasing music, as well as data analytics tools and music publishing services.

EmuBands: provides a simple but powerful digital music distribution service for artists, and record labels, to sell music online

TuneCore: One of the original DIY distributors, Tunecore users pay a one-off fee for the global distribution of single track or album releases. The platform also offers music publishing services.

Unlike record label or service deals, which traditionally report to artists and pay royalties on a twice-yearly basis, most DIY distributors will pay artists as soon as revenue is received from a digital service.

The downsides to a no frills DIY approach – aside from the lack of upfront finance – is that all the workload assumed by a label or service company will fall on the shoulders of the artist and their manager.

Ultimately, all this is a trade off, and artists and their managers have to determine which option works best for them and how it aligns with their shorter and long term goals and ambitions.

RECORD SHOPS & PHYSICAL MUSIC

With so much recorded music consumption moving to streaming, it's easy to forget physical formats like vinyl and CD. However, for certain types of artists, these can be an essential part of their business – as well as providing a potentially collectible object to sell at live shows and through record shops.

In fact, similar to local music venues, the support of local record shops should not be underestimated by music managers looking to build and develop an artist. Alongside regional radio and regional media, all are part of a vital grassroots network that nurtures emerging talent and provides opportunities to connect with the most dedicated audiences of music lovers.

As well as selling physical products, record shops also provide a fantastic opportunity to advertise shows and perform at instores, so making acquaintance with your local shop owner is definitely recommended!

Mastering and pressing a short-run of seven-inch singles is a fairly straightforward process these days, with a number of specialised companies offering this service from digital recordings – including repurposing of artwork for picture sleeves.

STARTING TO BUILD A FANBASE

Paul Craig, Nostromo Management & MMF Chair

"Building a passionate audience is fundamental to the success of an artist. Almost every manager remembers when their client was first playing shows and performing to a handful of people, and the thrill of returning to the same town or city and seeing a crowd start to grow. It's an incredible feeling, and vindication for all your hard work.

Picking up that momentum is absolutely critical, and it's vital that you hold onto these fans, communicate with them and look after them – whether that's giving them access to pre-sales, or interacting with them on social media, or providing exclusive content.

They'll often remain your most passionate supporters, and the kind of people who'll stick with an artist through thick and thin. Once you get those first 200 or so diehard fans, you can start to build a following and a proper business strategy."

Ultimately, the success and popularity of an artist, songwriter or producer will be dependent upon their music and art.

However, the long-term viability of their commercial business will rely upon growing, segmenting and expanding their audience.

In the analogue era, the majority of artists would start off by developing a local fanbase. They would perform at their local venue, target local media and pitch to their local radio station and local record shop, before looking to expand their audience regionally, then nationally and – if they were lucky enough – internationally.

Although these dynamics have remained ever-present – especially so in live music, where artists will still look to graduate upwards to higher-capacity venues and more prestigious support slots and festival bills – the shift to streaming and social media has enabled all artists to reach a global fanbase, lowered barriers to entry and led to 60k tracks a day being released on Spotify alone.

Helping artists develop and execute a strategy that will gain them attention, cut through the noise – and connect the dots between online and offline – is a fundamental part of the manager's role.

Typically this will involve a continual process of experimentation, with managers exploring different marketing techniques and processes as they go along, reviewing engagement and impacts.

Consequently, helping an artist to build and nurture their fanbase – freeing them to focus on creative aspects of their work – has become a core part of the manager's remit; and a remit that increasingly involves drawing upon the pools of consumer data generated from audio and video streaming, ticket purchases and social media activity.

The widespread availability of data, combined with the interconnectivity of online communications, has fundamentally changed how artists can interact with their audience, and most digital services offer specialised tools that allow artists to track consumption of their music and help increase that consumption through targeted promotion.

Whereas historically, artist-fan relationships were mostly filtered through intermediaries – such as record labels, retailers, broadcasters, the media and promoters – artists can now, in theory, build a direct connection to their audience. This is an incredibly powerful development.

Most managers will recommend that artists take ownership of their data at the earliest opportunity – for instance, by building a mailing list and owning their website – and continue to retain ownership of it.

The different kinds of consumer data from emails or social media, or streaming or ticketing is further discussed in Part Two of this book and are all outlined in detail in the MMF's Fan Data Guide, part of our ongoing Dissecting The Digital Dollar project.

THE ARTIST'S WEBSITE

A well-designed and fully-functioning website can act as a centrepoint for your artist's business – providing not only information (music, video, live shows, bio, photos, contacts, social media links) but also acting as a shop front with links to tickets, streaming and download sites, merchandise, vinyl and other physical product.

It can also offer another way of building your mailing list and collecting important fan data, such as email addresses and phone numbers.

Maintaining the website is therefore pretty important, as is ensuring that your artist retains full control of its ownership – especially if and when you start working with other partners.

There are a variety of off-the-shelf packages available to build and host a webpage (eg Squarespace, WIX), and most streaming platforms and download stores offer embeddable players – as do live music aggregators such as Bandsintown and Songkick which can provide links to touring schedules and ticketing agents.

Services like Mailchimp allow you to integrate mailing list functionalities and collect email addresses and other contact details.

TIPS FOR USING DATA & BUILDING A FANBASE FROM SCRATCH, SAMMY ANDREWS, CEO AND FOUNDER, DEVIATE DIGITAL

- *In terms of early-stage digital marketing you need to first understand how you want to present yourself and where. This must be authentic or it'll be dead in the water before you start. If you spend the time understanding the kinds of content that work for you it's far easier to generate income and sales.*

- *It's essential to understand data ownership vs usage. Always build your own database alongside any social networks and use social network followings to convert to your own database.*

  If you build a mailing list you own it, if you build a social network following you rent it. You'll want to utilise your database further collecting emails and phone numbers at every opportunity as well as having pixels in place across all your online presence. Don't ever hammer your database too often, instead get in touch with the right things at the right times and don't just shout at your social networking followers about release plans. Engage with them, ask questions, and allow a relationship to form between you and the fans.

- *Once you have an audience, use analytics to check where your fanbase are. This is essential infomation for tour routing, merchandise choices and paid spend on advertising.*

It's easy to assume everyone will like your music but they won't. Whilst it can be tempting to set ads up to go worldwide, this won't help you on a hyper-local level to build a fanbase in a specific area that will translate into say a healthy live/ touring business. Pick your priority territories (and cities) and stick to them in the first instance to build grounds swell. On a local level, be aware that if you use paid advertising to target audiences who are already being targeting by big paying advertisers you will pay over the odds to reach them. Try and profile your audience in a non-generic way so you can run test spends locally to see what/who resonates and build from there.

- *There are subtle differences between audiences of different genres in terms of where they are, how they interact online and what content resonates with them.*

Asking your acts to draw up a list of artists they believe they would be the ideal support act for can help and you can research to see the kinds of media and publications that cover these artists. Use that information as a jumping-off point to dig into wider marketing plans and profile your potential audience.

DIRECT TO FAN SERVICES

Once you have a fanbase, social media presence and a website, there are a range of opportunities for artists to sell music and other related products (e.g. t-shirts and merchandise) directly to their fanbase – either from bespoke web stores or via third-party "white label" services embedded on the artist website.

Some of the key services include:

Bandcamp: A service for independent artists who own all their rights, Bandcamp effectively acts as an online marketplace – allowing artists to create their own store and sell downloads, physical products and merchandise, as well as providing an embeddable streaming player. Artists set the prices and keep 82% of revenue. Bandcamp also offers a bespoke vinyl pressing service.

Music Glue: As well as creating and powering webstores for a host of major artists and labels, Music Glue also offers a "lite" service tier for self-releasing artists, allowing them to sell music, tickets and merchandise from a single bespoke shop. The platform also offers analytics alongside features to help collect fan data and build mailing lists.

Ochre: A technology platform that allows artists and labels to operate their own direct-to-consumer ecommerce operations. Ochre also offers warehousing and store management services.

Merchandise (Merch)

Similar to digital and physical music, there are a number of specialist ecommerce platforms that specialise in both creating and selling merchandise. These include the likes of terrible*, YourDesign, tshirtstudio, shirtinator, spreadshop, everpress and bonfire. Some of these companies will be capable of managing the entire merchandise supply chain from sourcing to delivery, as well as enabling e-commerce purchases online or at live shows. See more information about the environmental impact of merchandising and considerations for ethical suppliers in the section on climate action.

DEVELOPING LIVE PERFORMANCE

According to MMF research, live music is the most important revenue stream for the majority of artists generating on average 80% of earnings – and so, in the same breath, live music is also the most important revenue stream for the majority of managers, although probably not so much in the early days when it's more about building an audience and creating a buzz!

Expanding an artist's live business – helping them attract the support of agents, promoters and bookers, who will help propel their career forward – is a vital part of the manager's role.

In practice, most artists tend to build a career organically; performing at small grassroots venues and spaces in their home location and surrounding areas, developing their craft, before progressing further afield to bigger rooms and larger crowds.

Again, in the majority of cases, the overriding aim is to build momentum and attract a dedicated audience of ticket buyers capable of supporting a UK-wide tour, before exploring Europe, North America or other major music markets.

Many artists, and possibly most artists, keep to this organic trajectory – gradually moving up the live music ladder via support slots until they can secure headline appearances or festival bookings.

As a manager, you will undoubtedly view this progress symbiotically and in parallel with the other parts of your client's business – with other activities (e.g. new releases, prominent sync deals, brand tie-ins) feeding into and directing their touring and performing plans. The dynamics of online distribution have also accelerated this process, potentially increasing audience demand at a far earlier stage in an artist's career.

How a manager structures their client's live music business, and how much revenue they can potentially generate, is varied. Aside from an artist's popularity and talent, it can depend upon the genre they operate in, the cost and capacity of their production, and the number of individuals involved in putting that production on.

For instance, even in terms of transportation and accommodation costs, a DJ with their playlist downloaded to a memory stick or a solo performer with an acoustic guitar, will probably trump a seven-piece jazz band in terms of financial efficiency.

Equally, that seven-piece jazz band might enjoy certain openings and opportunities that won't be available to the DJ or solo troubadour – and vice versa.

So it's very much a case of "different strokes, for different folks". However, unlocking these opportunities, while establishing how you can invest in your artist in a sustainable way, can be a real challenge – especially in their early stage development, when live shows might barely cover expenses or operate at a loss.

By the time your artist is capable of selling tickets in their own right (what are sometimes called "hard tickets") then they'll probably start outsourcing some of the key responsibilities involved in putting on an event – for instance by working with a promoter, booking agent, a tour manager, or a live technician.

At this stage, the manager's remit will inevitably shift. Your focus will be to oversee these partnerships and manage a team, as well as working more closely with an accountant on budgets as your artist's touring becomes more complex.

These roles will be explored in more detail in Part Two, along with other necessities such as insurance, but we will start first with the fundamentals – planning and budgeting.

Your Touring Strategy

As with the other aspects of your client's career, from the get-go, it is important to take an initial assessment of where they are now with their live business, and where they want to progress – in both the short term and long term.

For instance, they might be playing regular shows in their immediate locality, but hold aspirations to tour nationally. Alternatively, they might want to perform at a specific venue or festival, or to play on the same line-up as one of their musical heroes tapping into ready made audiences. Or they might want to break new ground creatively, or to move beyond a certain scene or genre.

Initially it will be the manager's job to formulate a strategy with the artists as to how they will reach these objectives.

As part of this process, it is also important to understand why your artist is performing live in the first place.

Is it for financial reasons? Albeit, most early-stage touring makes very little money and breaks even at best.

Is it for publicity? Live shows offer an opportunity to connect with local press and radio, or to promote new music. In most instances, artists will also receive a small allocation of guest list tickets – providing an opportunity to invite guests or potential commercial partners.

Is it for development? Great performers are usually moulded over time. Through experience, they learn the art of stagecraft, and how to carry a show and captivate an audience. Most artists will start this process "under the radar" at small venues before graduating to bigger stages and more prestigious billing slots.

Is it to be active in the market? As an artist's career evolves, they will typically play tours to support a release cycle (i.e. if they have a new material being released) or to serve specific markets. Balancing audience demand is a careful consideration, and it is important not to oversaturate with ill-thought-out bookings. However, in the early stages of their career, many artists will perform constantly in order to build career momentum and gain experience.

Early stage roles of the manager in live music

Before your artist thinks about outsourcing certain key roles – for instance to a booking agent or a tour manager – they are likely to rely on their manager to keep their show on the road.

A manager's responsibilities might include:

Rehearsals

Any artist intending to perform before an audience will need to rehearse. Depending on the genre of music and the number of musicians involved in their set up, practice sessions can take part in almost any setting – from a spare room to the back of a pub – although many artists will inevitably end up using dedicated spaces where they can leave equipment, or where essentials like a PA, drum kit or microphones and mirrors are already set up. Professional rehearsal rooms are usually hired by the hour, although it may be possible to negotiate if you are booking for an extended period of time.

Getting Gigs

Most towns and cities in the UK have a dedicated venue for live music – whether that's a pub that regularly puts on live bands, or a local nightclub or arts venue. These will typically be the first port of call for artists looking to perform live, and many will have specific opportunities for upcoming acts – whether that's support slots, or evenings set aside specifically for new bands. They may be unpaid initially or for a share of the door but the more you can show you are building an audience for your artist the more that others in your scene are likely to notice you.

If your artist is not already performing at small local venues, it might be part of your remit to approach them and source performance opportunities – which might require details of your artist's credentials (eg a short biography, photo, social media, links to music), as well as evidence they can play and, ideally, pull in an audience.

Once your artist has some performances under their belt and evidence of gaining momentum, then it should be easier to expand their live activities and secure other performance opportunities further afield.

When playing an initial grassroots show, it is important to agree to any payment terms in advance and to have clear instructions about logistics – for instance, whether the venue has a PA or backline, and times for load-in and soundchecks.

Getting Paid

There are no hard and fast rules about what an artist will be paid for playing a show, and particularly so when they're just starting out or performing where entry is free or at a reduced price.

Another important factor, and often overlooked, is the number of people involved in the touring party. For example, a solo performer will enjoy certain economic advantages over a larger ensemble who need to transport their instruments and require the services of a roadie or sound technician.

In general, most aspects of live music are negotiable.

As a guideline, a brand new artist performing to ticket buyers in a 200-capacity venue locally is unlikely to earn much if their only draw initially is family and friends. Initially, promoters and venues will want to know how many fans you are likely to attract. On that basis, they might offer a guaranteed fee or a "door split" (dependent on how many people show up or buy tickets) or a combination of both. In either case, you should request advanced written confirmation of any fee as well as details of payment terms.

Do well and create a buzz and you may be offered support slots for bands touring through your town which may lead to a support tour. Support tours are notoriously badly paid (sometimes as low as £50 a gig) and often seen as a loss leader with that exclusive goal of creating an audience but think creatively, sometimes support bands can also provide the backing band for a solo artist helping subsidise wider costs of touring. Also if you do have leverage try to negotiate and figure out what equipment or transportation you can share to keep costs down. Some early level bands do swaps where they offer your artists a support slot in their home town where they can draw an audience and you do the same. Joint headline tours in this way can work well for artists with a strong regional audience trying to tour outside of there area. As always there are endless possibilities so think creatively.

Marketing

As well as booking shows, a manager might also be involved in the marketing and advertising of performances – for instance, by ensuring details are uploaded to an artist's website and social accounts, as well as live music aggregation / discovery platforms such as Songkick or Bandsintown. Managers increasingly look to negotiate ring-fenced budgets with promoters which they can use to promote local shows through the artists' socials.

Promotion can also be of the more hands-on variety – such as putting up posters in local record shops, pitching for interviews in local media or general word-of-mouth marketing.

Load in/Load out/Soundchecks

The 'load in' is the time when your artist is expected to arrive and "load in" their gear. They need to remove it at "load out". You should agree to clear instructions of both entry and exit before the show, and ensure your artist has this information. Similarly, you should be provided with clear times about soundchecks and ensure that the sound levels are agreed – both on stage in the monitors, and offstage via the mixing desk.

PRS for Music

To ensure songwriters are paid for performance of their works, PRS for Music charges a tariff on all live music events and DJ sets. At larger events, PRS receive a percentage of ticket sales (currently 4.2% of box office receipts) and require that promoters, event organisers and venues collect and submit setlist data – enabling the songwriters of the works performed to be paid.

For small grassroots live shows, PRS operates a flat fee Gigs & Clubs scheme (currently £10 per event) which is theoretically distributed between the writers whose songs are being performed.

Understandably, if an artist is performing their own music, this system requires them to register their compositions to PRS in advance. If the writers cannot be located or the works are not registered, then the unmatched revenue collected by PRS is retained for a certain period before being reallocated.

Live Mailing List

Playing shows is a great way for an artist to start building a database of fans – even if you're simply collecting names via pen and paper. Aside from seeking permission to contact audience members in the future, collecting email addresses, mobile numbers and social media accounts can provide an invaluable foundation for your artist's business, allowing them to start alerting potential fans about upcoming shows and releases.

Merchandise

Aside from door revenue (i.e. a cut of ticket sales) and PRS royalties, live shows offer artists an opportunity to sell merchandise and other physical goods, such as T-shirts, CDs and vinyl. Watch out for venue commissions which can be up to 25% of gross and severely impact artists' take home income. Check out the FAC's 100% venues campaign for a list of venues which don't charge commission.

Creating a Tour Budget

Perhaps the most important role for the manager. Whether an artist is performing in the back room of pubs or on the largest arena stages, you'll need to create and oversee a budget.

As touring grows more complex, then an accountant is invariably involved in this process, but even at a small scale – in fact *especially* at a small scale – there's no getting around the inbuilt costs of performing live, whether that's paying out for practice rooms, instruments and equipment hire, travel and subsistence expenses, or advertising and marketing.

Compounding this situation, the financial return from live music is likely to be quite minimal at first and probably break even at best. As your artist progresses to larger venues and bigger events, they will undoubtedly incur additional costs, such as insurance, tour management, road crew or sound engineers.

Live Music Budgets: The Unpredictable vs the Unmovable.
One indisputable fact around live music is that while revenues are unpredictable, the costs of performing are immovable – albeit the most skilled managers are those who can balance the aspirations of their artist, while delivering a show at the most efficient and effective cost!

Drawing up a simple spreadsheet showing profit and loss is incredibly easy, and a great way of teaching yourself how to plan.

In essence, budgeting can be done in two different ways, either (1) adding up the costs and outlays per show and establishing how much revenue you'll need to make from ticket and merchandise sales to make it affordable; or (2) working out your potential show revenue, and then working backwards to establish your necessary costs, and areas where efficiencies could be made.

In these early stages of development, your budget / information sheet will be quite rudimentary – detailing transport and accomodation costs, the times and locations of the performance, and the agreed fee.

The process becomes more complex as your artist advances and starts playing bigger and more complex events. However, it's common sense to start developing good habits, such as having important agreements in writing – including how much you will be commissioning for your time and expertise.

As we'll soon discuss, the dynamics of live music can, on occasion, put the artist and the manager in a far more financially perilous position than others involved in a show – and many of the outsourced roles (eg tour manager, booking agent) have far greater certainty in what they'll get paid.

Although probably too detailed for early stage artists, the MMF provides its members with an incredibly useful budget template that can easily be adapted and simplified. If you are a member you can access this in the resources section of the website.

TIPS FOR GETTING AN ARTIST'S LIVE BUSINESS OFF THE GROUND

"I use targeted social media and digital marketing to increase regional ticket sales and core fanbases. Seeing the gigs as a means to promote the music, and the music as a means to promote the gigs has been effective in building loyal followings that we can grow the rest of the artists business around, and continue to develop an audience with or without the support of traditional media."

Stephen Archibald – JUMPING THE SHARK MGMT

"When you've played an amazing show, fans will never be more eager to see you again. Always have something on sale ready for the next event so that you can continuously stay in the consciousness of your audience. Do underplays that sell quickly and create the demand. There will be a time to turn the dial and be ambitious, but hopefully by that point you will have taught fans to get tickets early using this strategy."

Callum Reed – Touchdown Management

"Having a well respected and connected agent, makes it much easier to navigate the live market. This, coupled with a collaborative approach and great understanding of the artists music and vision for their career can be key to sourcing and maximising live opportunities. What you say no to can be just as important as what you say yes to so, a good understanding of who the artists audience is or should be is essential to ensuring resources are not wasted and artists are not demoralised."

Cleo Amedume – Muvva Management

CHAPTER 3

Creating Opportunities: Promotion & Marketing

B y default, artists are involved in the marketing and promotion process from the minute they upload music or activate a social media account.

However, at these initial stages likely that you as a manager will pick up responsibility to oversee their promotion strategy – rather than spending resources on PR and marketing specialists. Being skilled and aware of managing small digital marketing campaigns is a must for managers with platforms allowing micro investments and specific audience targeting through business management and backend tools.

More than that, as the primary champion of your artist, you will be looking to create opportunities – whether through networking and building relationships, approaching media, looking to book live shows or attempting to get your client's music on playlists.

Some basic questions to ask before starting any of this outreach work:

What is our target?
How do we get there?

Who do I need to contact?

Who might be able to help?

What assets will I need?

What preparations will I need to do?

BUILDING NETWORKS & SHOWCASING

Another key aspect of management is to build and then continue expanding your industry networks – finding and interacting with potential partners who can help your artist achieve their goals, whether that's on a creative or commercial basis.

One fast track to achieving this is by joining the MMF and connecting to a ready-made community of music managers as well as other people in the industry and to build relationships.

Similarly, there are a range of music business conferences around the UK which also act as showcase opportunities for artists. If you manage producers or songwriters they can also be a great place to pick up new collaborations and potential clients.

The Great Escape, for instance, which is the UK's biggest showcase for new music, offers performance slots to more than 450 artists from across the world.

These events can be invaluable for both managers and their artists, and provide a perfect opportunity to invite along potential supporters or business partners. However, to make the most of showcasing, you can't just rely on people turning up on a whim.

For a manager, preparation is vital. For instance, by checking out delegate and speaker lists to see who is attending, contacting relevant individuals in advance to organise meetings and inviting them to attend your artist's event, updating your artist's social accounts, and ensuring their showcase is listed on the event website or promotional materials.

The process of actually registering your artist's interest in performing is usually straightforward, however you should expect to demonstrate their credentials (e.g. proof of media interest, radio plays, streaming data, ticket sales) in order to secure a favourable slot – or any slot at all.

For these reasons, showcasing should ideally be built into your business plan – with the aim of applying strategically for specific shows only when your artist has reached appropriate staging posts.

We will cover overseas showcasing in subsequent chapters.

In other scenarios, it is also commonplace for managers to arrange private showcases in rehearsal rooms, studios or online for invited industry guests. A number of talent development showcases – such as iluvlive, Karousel and Gold Dust – also provide a bridge between the promotion of new talent and industry audiences.

Some of the key UK based conferences and showcases include:

The Great Escape
A 3-day festival held in Brighton in May. TGE presents a huge range of new music showcases for upcoming artists, as well as a highly regarded conference strand featuring both UK and international speakers.

Sound City
Another well-established music industry conference and new music showcase, with the main edition taking place across 3 days in Liverpool and Ipswich (typically in April/May) and with a smaller event in Ipswich (typically in October).

Wide Days
Established in 2010, the Edinburgh-based Wide Days takes place over 3 days in May, combining a conference strand with showcases from mostly Scottish artists.

Focus Wales
An annual three-day showcase and conference event for the Welsh music industry. Takes place in Wrexham.

BBC Introducing Live
Usually taking place in October/November, Introducing Live typically features a wide range of speakers representing all sectors of the business.

The Ultimate Seminar
Co-founded by MMF vice-chair Kwame Kwaten, the Ultimate Seminar is a well-established day event in London, where some of the industry's biggest names speak before a room of aspiring young music entrepreneurs.

ILMC
The International Live Music Conference was founded over 30 years ago, and widely recognised as one the world's most prominent gatherings of live music professionals. Taking place in March, ILMC is an invite-only event, and new attendees need to be nominated by two existing delegates.

Brighton Music Conference
The UK's foremost electronic music conference taking place in May.

English Folk Expo Showcase
Annual showcase of UK folk and roots music, taking place in annually in October.

Showcase Scotland
Aimed at furthering the live export opportunities for Scottish based artists working in the genres of folk, traditional, Scots, Gaelic, world and acoustic music.

MEDIA FOR ARTISTS

The range of music-related media is vast, and covers everything from amateur blogs through to genre-specialist titles, as well as local, national and international press – plus radio, podcasts, UGC platforms and TV.

However, when starting from scratch, your initial aim will likely be to locate and connect with tastemakers (e.g. journalists, music supervisors, DJs influencers, or playlister curators) in the media who you believe will have affinity with your client and their music.

Before contacting anyone, it will always pay to do your research and prepare. Sending a handful of well-thought-out personalised emails or messages will always be better than blanket bombing potential supporters.

It would also pay dividends to consider the following:

- What story are you looking to tell about your artist?
- What makes them interesting and stand out? Why are they worthy of anyone's attention?
- Do you have photos, links to music – ideally uploaded to a streaming service – and other assets (eg video)?
- Have you written a short succinct bio? This should outline who your artist is, their achievements, and any current or upcoming activity – eg live shows, new releases.
- Can you make a list of journalists and DJ's who might be potential supporters? For instance, those who specialise in the genre of your artist, or have given coverage to artists similar to them.
- Do you know how to contact them?
- What outcome are you looking for? For instance, are you encouraging them to listen to some music, write a review or attend a show?

For an unknown artist, getting the attention of major publications that receive hundreds of press releases and pitches each week will undoubtedly be challenging. It can be tough to stand out.

Therefore it often pays dividends to think locally or specifically first, and approach blogs, websites that specialise in covering new music, first. Once you gain momentum and start generating up support for your artist, then you can use this as leverage to generate further coverage.

MUSIC VIDEOS

These days, music is increasingly an audio-visual medium. Video has become an incredibly important way for artists to tell their stories, to promote themselves and to build an audience.

The costs of making and distributing video content is no longer prohibitive, and there are countless examples of artists generating significant online audiences and viewer counts for relatively small budgets. (Although, as with other aspects of your artist's work, if you as a manager are investing your own time and money in their video productions, then this should be incorporated into your commercial partnership and commissioning structure.)

With user-upload platforms such as YouTube, TikTok and Twitch all attracting huge global audiences, it is imperative for most artists that they establish and control their own channels, that they have a strategy to service those channels with creative content, and that they can either generate revenue from that content or utilise it as a source of data.

YouTube have an extremely helpful set-up page for Creators that illustrates some of the key considerations when setting up a personalised channel, including editorial tips ("Establish Your Voice", "Customise Your Channel Branding", "Get Set Up With A Production Plan") as well as advice on creating playlists, using data analytic tools and growing an audience.

TikTok offers a similar Creator Marketplace, while Twitch has its own Creator Camp.

Beyond these UGC platforms there are also a multitude of video-based blogs and websites – for instance SB:TV, LinkUp TV, GRM Daily, Colours – while most music media will also host their own bespoke video channels.

MANAGER TIPS ABOUT MAKING VIDEOS FROM SCRATCH FROM THE ACCELERATOR CLASS OF 2020

"Learning Photoshop and Premiere Pro is an essential manager skill and many tools have free trial periods available."

Jazz Rocket, 67 Artists

"Have a strong creative idea and work with other emerging talent – collaborate."

Ammena Badley – the Ko-lab

"Visualisers are essential additional content and 4K royalty free footage can be found from sites such as pexels.com."

Andrew Ellis, Aery Music

RADIO & BBC INTRODUCING

While there are relatively few barriers to entry when it comes to uploading music to a streaming service, getting played on the radio represents more of a serious proposition – not only for the kudos and promotion it offers, but also for the performance revenues.

While there are number of highly regarded online radio stations (eg NTS, Worldwide FM, Soho Radio) and some of the UK's commercial networks do offer genre specialist programming which is open to emerging artists, one of the easier routes into radio is via BBC Introducing – a bespoke platform established in 2007, that allows unsigned artists to upload their music and be considered for plays on local BBC stations and BBC Sounds, as well as opening opportunities at BBC events.

Effectively, it is a great way to start building your artist's profile and developing a track record. Many current A-list or B-list artists started their journey via BBC Introducing.

STREAMING PLAYLISTS

For many artists, alongside a play on national radio, having their tracks added to the biggest and most popular playlists on the major streaming services is perceived as the Holy Grail — providing not only hugely valuable exposure, but also helping generate revenue.

All the major streaming services offer a combination of "official" playlists (eg "New Music Friday" on Spotify, or "Today's Hits" on Apple Music) alongside an endless variety of branded or user-created playlists.

Official 'own-brand' playlists all have well-established mechanisms for artists to pitch.

For instance, Spotify's process demands that artist's send music directly to editors via *Spotify For Artists* — with tracks needing to be uploaded and submitted at least 7 days before release date for consideration. Only one track is allowed per release, and artists are also required to submit artwork, as well as a biography, and details about genre, lyrics, credits and so on. There's more details at Spotify for Artists.

Similarly, Apple Music offers a portal called Apple Music For Artists, which also includes information about using Apple's music making software (eg Logic Pro and Garageband) as well as spatial audio; YouTube Music has YouTube For Artists portal, which includes expert advice on video uploads, Deezer's portal is called Deezer for Creators, while Amazon Music offers Amazon for Artists.

As well as helping artists promote and pitch their music, all these portals offer data analytic tools, enabling managers and artists to track music consumption, as well as marketing tips and advice on revenue generation.

These types of professional services are also replicated across social platforms such as SoundCloud Pro Unlimited, TikTok's Creator Portal, Instagram for Creators, Twitch's Creator Dashboard or Snap's Creator Hub.

When it comes to playlists, many managers will try to build direct relationships with decision makers at DSPs — albeit, if you work with a record label or other recording partner further down the line, then they will often pitch for playlists as part of their digital marketing efforts.

However, it's becoming increasingly essential that managers can build relationships with editors and playlist curators, most of whom are passionate music fans in their own right.

TIPS FOR MARKETING ON STREAMING SERVICES AND PLAYLISTS

"Make sure you are clear which genre / sub genre your artist belongs to and send over a clear background head & shoulders portrait photo for potential playlist covers. Playlists are curated by real editors who need to develop personal relationships with the artists they work with. Help raise their profile by tagging them and the DSP into social posts."

Sarah M, Muise Management

"If you're able to speak directly to a DSP, have a clear 3-6 month plan of what's confirmed regarding features, shows and moments that are planned for your release."

**Shikayla Nadine, SNM Management/
Lateral Management**

"Building relationships across all the DSPs is continuing to be important, streaming is a great thing for the industry. Getting artists properly paid for it will be a continuing ambition of all managers. I would really like to see that move along in the years to come."

Craig Jennings, Raw Power Management

As always, finding people who love your artist's music as much as you do is the goal.

Whilst editorial and algorithmic plays only make up between 10-30% of a streaming platform's content they are influential and important for exposure and tipping artists. User driven personal playlists, discovery from other media and sharing is still the main way music is consumed and thinking about your whole marketing strategy is the best way to drive streams and playlist potential.

SOCIAL MEDIA & SOCIAL CHANNELS

Social media, if they choose to use it, offers artists a platform to communicate in their own authentic voice – either as individuals or as part of a group. When taking on a new client it may be wise for you both to review their social media history to see if there is anything particularly contentious they may have published in their past so you can discuss how to handle this and also help advise and guide them in the future on their public posts.

As a manager, you might also be permitted access to these accounts, as might other business partners – especially if they are used primarily as commercial or information channels, it is vital that your client retains overall control and ownership of any soci al media channels they intend to use – including video channels such as YouTube, TikTok and Twitch, but it is important that ownership is not given away as it provides the primary channel for fan engagement.

Building a following from scratch takes time and effort, and can be incredibly valuable. Your artist should be conscious of this, and the power and immediacy that social media can bring.

How artists use their social channels is very much down to the individual. Some enjoy having direct personal contact with audiences and embrace using sites like TikTok and Instagram as part of their marketing activity. Others will want to avoid them completely!

What's most important is that you discuss how your artist wants to communicate, on which platforms, and with what regularity.

It's also important to set boundaries. The concept of "digital burnout" which we discuss further in Part Two, and the ever-increasing demands to feed social media is becoming a subject of significant debate within the music business – with many stepping back because of the adverse impact on their mental health.

TIPS FOR MANAGING AN ARTIST'S SOCIAL MEDIA CHANNELS AND GETTING THE MOST OUT OF THEM

1. Get the same profile handles across all platforms
2. Set up cross posting wherever possible
3. Have a schedule if possible for key regular content management
4. Keep up to date with trends and popular hashtags, many of the social media companies have specific artist newsletters or best practice guides
5. Get someone else to do it! Investing in a specialist company can really help in the long term

Yasin El Ashrafi
BEM founder
& owner, HQ
Familia

CHAPTER 4

Support & Funding

SUPPORT & FUNDING FOR MANAGERS

As a member of the Music Managers Forum (MMF) you instantly become part of the world's biggest community of professional music managers. We offer an established network through which managers can share experiences, opportunities and information. Our core goals are to:

- **Educate:** We support managers' continuous professional development within an evolving music industry.
- **Innovate:** We create and highlight opportunities to develop and grow artist businesses.
- **Advocate:** We provide a collective voice and leadership to affect change for a transparent and fairer music industry for artists and their fans.

With membership fees from as little as £60 per year for the under 30s and £100 + VAT for over 30s, the MMF's operations are also supported by our Associate partners, who range from leading digital music services such as Spotify, YouTube

Music, TikTok and Amazon Music, through to start-ups, accountancy services, legal firms and a number of other music-related businesses.

Our members have exclusive access to regular seminars, training and networking events. The MMF also has its own education programme including the highly recommended Essentials of Music Management, as well as social events and our annual Artist & Manager Awards.

You can find out more and sign up to join us on our website www.themMF.net

**Nim Jani,
Catalyst
Management**

"For someone without any formal qualification in music, I am sometimes faced with the question 'am i doing this right?'. Through all my conversations with the MMF, I've felt like the job that I've created is respected. I'm treated the same as someone who may have 40 years experience and 50 platinum records. My self-engineered workflow churned out from my vision and dreams suddenly is given validation from like-minded people who have the time of day to listen. The MMF is way more than the Music Managers Forum, for me it's become a place to know it's not only me going through this, actually we're figuring it all out together."

**Diane Wagg,
Deluxxe
Management,
Custodian and
former MMF
Chair**

"Over its 30 years, the MMF has been instrumental in changing the music industry for the better and developing the craft of quality artist management. During that period, I've been involved at every level, from being an impassioned member to becoming Chair, and in my current position as Custodian. The collective and collaborative action of MMF members, sharing knowledge and vocalising their concerns and dreams for the industry, is impressive – always placing the artist and manager in conversations where they were previously overlooked or bypassed. The MMF fights firmly and fairly, placing evidence centrally at the heart of its campaigns. Together we've uncovered the real issues around the lack of transparency in streaming, we've pressed Governments about the importance of music exports, and we've diversified our community by improving access to funding, education and training."

ACCELERATOR PROGRAMME FOR MUSIC MANAGERS

Since 2019, the MMF has operated a groundbreaking grants and training initiative specifically for Music Managers. Supported by YouTube Music, Arts Council England, the Scottish Music Industry Association and Creative Scotland, the year-long programme aims to support and empower talented independent managers and to help put their businesses on a more sustainable footing – offering grants of up to £15,000 as well as weekly expert-led training and networking sessions.

Accelerator has resulted in a wide range of successes, including new record and publishing deals, new brand and live music partnerships, as well as Top Ten singles and albums and nominations for talent from The Mercury Awards, Grammys, MOBOs and Brit Awards. Importantly, it has helped expand horizons and significantly widen the MMF's network – ensuring we have a pool of the best emerging managers joining our membership each year.

More details about Accelerator and how to apply can be found on our website.

MANAGER EDUCATION & NETWORKS

As well as building your network of contacts, a good manager should remain abreast of industry developments, new technologies and trends. You can't be an expert in everything, but a working knowledge of the commercial landscape and how it might provide opportunities for your artist is important.

As with networking, membership of the MMF can fulfil many of your educational needs – and as well as regular expert-led training events and insight sessions with our Associates, we also run the ever popular two-day Essentials of Music Management course that provides a one-stop introduction to music management.

MMF's Mechanics of Music Management includes sessions on the Role of the Music Manager, Managing an Artist Business, Making Money from Music Copyright, Record Deals and Label Services, Music Publishing and Publishing Deals, and Building, Growing and Managing a Fanbase. Additionally, MMF often collaborates with consultancy companies such as CMU Insights and Music Ally, both of whom offer regular and specialised training courses.

There are also a number of well-respected magazines and websites dedicated to different aspects of the music business, including:

Music Week
The longest-running magazine dedicated to the UK's music business. Music Week now publishes as a monthly print magazine, as well as a news website.

"In my experience, networking is everything in artist management. Early on in your career, building and nurturing a 'living database' of peers, mentors and reliable service providers creates the most solid foundation for thriving in the long term. And of course, for many artists managers are 'only as strong as your contacts' with labels, agents, promoters etc. So developing those relationships and continuing to nurture them is crucial."

Stephen Budd, Stephen Budd Music Limited and former MMF Chair

Record of the Day
For subscribers, RotD offers a daily breakdown of all the most relevant music related news – as well as a weekly PDF round-up of industry developments.

CMU
Free to access, CMU provides a daily rundown of the biggest music business stories.

Music Ally
Focussed predominantly on the digital music business, Music Ally provides a morning round-up of news stories for subscribers as well as bi-weekly reports.

Music Business Worldwide
Free to access, MBW takes a global focus on the music business, with a daily editorial of news stories, interviews and features.

Billboard
Subscription only, Billboard is predominantly focussed on the US music business.

HITS
Free to access, HITS is also predominantly US-focused.

Trapital
A free weekly memo on a mission to elevate hip-hop culture.

IQ
Subscription only, IQ focuses on the UK and international live music business. The monthly print edition is complemented by daily online news updates.

Pollstar
Free to read online, Pollstar is predominantly focussed on the US live music business.

SUPPORT & FUNDING FOR ARTISTS

While Accelerator is the world's only bespoke funding programme for music managers, there are multiple funding opportunities available for artists and songwriters – for example, through industry sources like the PRS Foundation, the UK's leading funder of new music and talent development, charities like Help Musicians, Youth Music or from Arts Council England, Creative Scotland, the Arts Council of Wales or the Arts Council of Northern Ireland.

Alongside these funds and more the traditional advances offered by record labels, distributors or music publishers, we are now also seeing the emergence of bespoke investment companies like beatBread who use data analytics as a basis to offer upfront payments to independent artists in return for a percentage of their streaming revenues over a fixed time period. With streaming capable of delivering more predictable and measurable flows of income to artists, it is likely we will see more of these kinds of innovations in the future.

Early career funding opportunities are also available for managers and artists to apply for development of music and delivery events and tours as well as from a number of talent development organisations which often focus in either a geographical or genre area.

ADVICE ON PREPARING FOR FUNDING – LIZA BUDDY, CHAOS AND BEDLAM

- *Make a plan to identify the type of funding you want*

  Bullet point a 1-2 year development plan for all your clients, pinpointing the areas you believe funding will be required. This will help you identify where the shortfalls might be, and help your decision-making about which funds to apply for. Funds can be specific only wanting to support one area for example recording, releasing, touring, showcasing or export. Others focus on creative development, collaborations or community projects or even certain age groups or other demographics.

  When you've identified the fund you want to apply for, plan ahead and check for any submission deadlines.

- *Finding/sourcing funding*

  Help Musicians host a Funding Wizard on their website which is an excellent resource. You should also explore your regional Arts council and research what kind of organisations and individuals have previously been granted funding.

- *Prepping for the application*

  Bullet point the following key information, which is generic to most applications. This can be invaluable when drafting proposals:

  1 Career achievements across live shows, radio, press and recordings and live and online audience figures

  2 Describe the project you require funding for – your artist biog or company mission is a good starting point

  3 Think about clear goals – you want to reach through this project and how you are you going to achieve these goals

  4 Describe both your current and potential audience

  5 Calculate the current income vs expenses of the artist's business

Things to look out for;

Eligibility/Criteria – check that your artist/project fits with the funding requirements

Deadlines – check whether there is a fixed or rolling submission deadline. You should expect around 6–10 weeks to find out whether your application has been successful, and be aware that there might be a further delay until you actually receive any funds so planning ahead is essential.

Reporting – If you are successful you will need to report your project results and final expenses. As a manager, it is vital you keep on top of this during the project period. Keeping proper accounts will also help you track career growth and potentially help with future funding applications.

Know your worth – Arts Council National Lottery Project Grants allows you to include a Project Managers Fee within your expenses, while the PPL Momentum Music Fund allows you to add on a Manager Cost.

As well as any monetary benefit, receiving funding is also a stamp of credibility – it can raise awareness around an artist and open doors to other sources of finance. Funders need applicants and love to explore ways in which they can raise the profile of both your work so always credit funders as agreed.

MENTAL HEALTH AND WELL BEING – TAKING CARE OF YOURSELF AND YOUR ARTISTS

The music business has always been stressful and exhausting, especially for a young and inexperienced manager. In the current environment, the demands have increased exponentially. There is always too much to do, and it's easy to start feeling removed from the love of music that got you here in the first place.

You won't be alone in this, and as highlighted in the MMF's Code of Practice it's vitally important to pay attention to both your own mental health and those of your clients. Be aware of your legal responsibilities in safeguarding effectively what is a work environment and be conscious if consuming alcohol or other substances that this can impair judgement and potentially lead to business liabilities.

To assist our membership, in 2021 the MMF updated our Guide To Mental Health – a free-to-download publication, co-authored with Sam Parker of specialist mental health consultants at The Parker Consultancy, that is specifically tailored to the well-being concerns of modern day music managers.

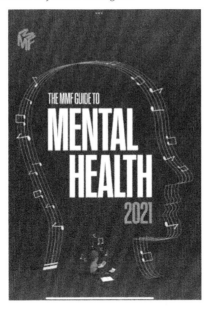

The guide includes detailed chapters on areas including Stress Management, Imposter Syndrome, Anxiety & Depression and Alcoholism & Drug Dependency, and provides a full directory of professional support services and signposting to further information and resources.

WHAT TIPS WOULD YOU GIVE A YOUNGER MANAGER ABOUT LOOKING AFTER THEIR OWN MENTAL HEALTH AND THOSE OF THEIR CLIENTS?

Sumit Bothra, Managing Director, ATC management

"Handling the psychological well-being of our artists, our team members, ourselves, and our families is one of any manager's biggest challenges. At no other point in human history have we been as globally connected and hyper-exposed to each other as we are now. This data-measured connectivity puts us all on one type of scoreboard or another – most often based on wealth, power, influence, impact, success, or popularity.

As managers we are expected to take our care for others seriously and this includes being attentive to how these factors influence the self-worth of those in our care. Are we properly equipped to help others as well as ourselves? Do we lean on each other when the going gets tough? Do we learn honestly from tragedy or mistakes? These are the tough questions we need to ask ourselves and address.

The MMF Mental Health Guide is a vital resource for managers and their teams, as are industry wide resources such as the Music Minds Matter helpline. Being open and honest about challenges in this area will help bring about early solutions, build trust, and assist the artist and manager in creating long-term, sustainable, and healthy careers together."

This brings us to the end of Part One. At this point, with a bit of luck, your client is starting to gain traction, revenue is starting to flow, and you are moving towards establishing a formal artist-management agreement.

In other words, when business is happening then you're acting like a business!

But, having assumed a potentially significant workload, this will now be the point that you look to start devolving responsibilities and build a team – probably starting with a lawyer and an accountant.

How you build a team and develop these partnerships is the focus of the second section of this book.

PART 2

*Growing Your Management
Business*

I f the first part of this book was focussed on the fundamentals of music management, and starting a management company – this second part will explore the process of expanding your business and building the partnerships and networks that will enable your artist to grow and thrive.

To reiterate the themes of Part One, most managers when they start out are likely to be poorly resourced, and juggling a multitude of other jobs. According to MMF research, the majority end up doing a bit of everything – which eventually amounts to a hell of alot.

On the plus side, this can be an incredible way of expanding your knowledge about the music business. In an industry where many people gain experience in a specific silo, this can open up opportunities further down the line.

However, as soon as your artist starts to gain traction, such working practices are unlikely to be long term sustainable. At this point, you'll need to think about bringing in outside expertise and building and managing a team.

Or you might consider restructuring your business to partner with another manager, or to work under the umbrella of a larger management company where you can tap into their resources and expertise.

This requires an altogether different skill set. Rather than taking on responsibilities, you'll frequently be devolving work and overseeing a multitude of moving parts

For instance, if you help secure a recording deal for your artist, then the record label or label service company will likely wish to assume responsibility for relationships with retailers and DSPs, as well as lead on responsibility for release campaigns and marketing. Similarly, a music publisher might be expected to take on the administrative burden of dealing with collecting societies or pitching for sync opportunities.

They are specialists, and these are areas they specialise in.

In this scenario, the manager's role will increasingly be to liaise with these partners, to ensure they're doing what they're contracted to do and performing to expectations, and – importantly – that the team is pulling in the same direction.

In an ideal world, an artist's recorded activity should help feed and grow their live and direct-to-fan business – and vice versa.

Because a manager should have oversight across all parts of the artist's business, they are in the unique position to formulate a unified campaign strategy that connects the dots. A good manager is also likely to take a longer-term career outlook than other partners, some of whom may be working with multiple artists and driven by more short-term motivations.

At times, overseeing these relationships will create tension, with the manager often having to protect and guide the artist where they can, and oversee competing demands from different partners.

Such a time of transition is also when managers can feel vulnerable — where the relationship with your client becomes formalised, where you agree legal binding boundaries, and where the commercial structures of your business become more complex.

For independent managers there can also be the fear of your artist being tempted to leave, or move on to a more established company.

Like any relationship, there is always the potential of a breakdown, and, where possible, some sort of contingency plan should be in place for this eventuality. Regardless of any personal connection or feelings towards your client, it is recommended that your artist / manager contract is legally agreed — including a settlement agreement or sunset clause if you decide to part ways.

In other words, this is a time when the dynamics of your business are likely to be tested — along with your resilience, your negotiating powers and your delegating talents.

This is also when you'll probably start building the profile and reputation as a manager — making yourself more visible on sites like LinkedIn, creating a website that outlines your services, and potentially attracting the attention of media or conference organisers.

CHAPTER 5

Accountants and Lawyers

s highlighted in Part One, most managers when starting out will not rush into a formal partnership with their client. Although they may have a verbal or short term agreement about roles, responsibilities and commissions, in all likelihood they won't have a written contract in place but will embark on a trial period.

However, once your artist starts generating revenues and your working relationship becomes established, it'll be time to move that relationship forward and employ the services of a lawyer to formalise a contract.

This will clarify the services you provide as manager, how you invoice for those services, and what activities might be considered as expenses.

Although some managers will put off signing a contract with their client – and a few will never sign a contract with their client – the MMF strongly recommends that you do put pen to paper and put your relationship on the strongest possible legal footing.

There are a number of reasons for this, but primarily:

1 **Security & Clarity** A contract will provide a legal foundation to your commercial relationship and wrap it in a specific time period. For instance, if you are charging a 20% commission for your services, then the contract should outline what revenue you'll actually be commissioning on.

For instance, will you be taking 20% of any label advance? Will you be taking 20% of the PPL and PRS revenue?

Will you commission the gross of your artist's live income? Or only on the profit, after show costs are taken out? The latter practice is far more common in the UK, while the former is typical in North America.

If you are entering into any joint ventures with your artist, or offering services outside of management – for instance, you might be running the label that releases their recordings, or running the publishing company that administers their copyrights or acting as a tour manager or agent- then a contract can also provide definitions to these boundaries.

Similarly, a contract should set out a clear duration for your professional relationship – which might be based on a certain time period (5 years is common, with specific break clauses inserted along the way) or within an album or release cycle.

In short, a contract should offer peace of mind that an artist is committed to working with you for a stated period of time.

2 **Post-term Commission**. All artist-manager contracts should also contain what is called a "sunset clause". This will establish how you are paid when your professional relationship ends (either when your contract ran its course, or it was terminated) and set out a commission structure for work completed during your agreement – for instance on recordings, compositions and productions. Effectively, the "sunset clause" helps offset the risk and investment made by the manager especially as there may be little to no earnings in the first few years of artists development but the money may start to flow 3-5 years into a career when the manager is no longer with the artist but laid the groundwork for that success.

The duration of sunset clauses can vary, although it is typical to simply double the length of the artist-manager contract. A few managers earn commission in perpetuity on the projects they worked on as they argue that the producer, mixer, label, and the A&Rs usually do likewise. In practice, most post-term commission is rarely beyond 10 years, and the rate of commission will often gradually decrease – e.g. it might be set at 20% for 5 years, and then come down in increments until it reaches zero. However, given the difficulty in managers ensuring they get paid this commission many are looking at different forms of management agreements and rights ownership as part of development deals for brand new artists, especially when they are investing time and money without remuneration upfront.

Ideally, your contract will spell out quite clearly what activities you are permitted to commission against post-term. For instance, if your artist re-records a track that was released under the scope of your contract, you probably wouldn't be able to claim commission on the new recording, but you could probably do so for any song royalties generated.

AT WHAT POINT SHOULD A MANAGER FORMALISE AN AGREEMENT WITH THEIR ARTIST?

"A 6 month trial is a good opportunity for both sides to get to know each other."

Adam Tudhope, Everybody's

"As soon as both the artist, their lawyer and the manager are comfortable with doing so."

Brian Message, Co-Chair ATC Management

Crucially, when agreeing an artist/manager contract, both you and your artist will need separate legal representation. This is the one occasion when you will be on opposite sides of the negotiating table, and therefore it is imperative you both have your own independent legal advice. If your artist does not have independent legal advice then any post-term agreement could potentially be challenged, meaning you could work with a client for years for little to no return, and then just as their career properly takes off as a result, if your contract ends, you would then earn nothing for the time you had invested.

As we've already reiterated, there is no such thing as a "standard" artist-manager contract. However, for the benefit of upcoming managers and artists, the MMF, FAC and Musicians' Union have created an "example contract" that we fully recommend you download and familiarise yourself with.

How Much Does This Cost?

Drawing up an artist-manager contract should not be hugely onerous and expensive, and many lawyers will be incentivised to offer discounted fixed rates in order to retain the long-term business of such key clients, including managers whom they hope to have returning business from.

However, costs vary and are negotiable but can increase if your business is more complex – for instance, if it involves joint ventures, production deals or partnerships where problems might be more difficult to resolve if your relationship breaks down. Managers will also have to negotiate or consider how the client will meet the legal fees for their independent consultation with a lawyer and how this will be paid for often making a contribution for both sides expenses if they must to secure a client.

THE IMPORTANCE OF MANAGER AND LAWYER RELATIONSHIPS

It is always recommended that you build a relationship with a lawyer for your own management business. However, once you have a written agreement with your artist, it is likely that you will then develop a close relationship with their lawyer – and ideally, going forward, all of you will be working towards the same ends, to help grow, evolve and expand the artist's business.

Whenever your artist enters a contractual partnership – for instance, with a record label, a publisher, or a live agent – their lawyer would be expected to offer independent legal advice. Their core purpose is to help ensure that their client gets the best deal possible.

However, their role as part of the artist's core team is likely to run far deeper than this.

For a start, most respected law firms will be plugged into all aspects of the industry – in addition to artists, songwriters, producers and managers, their clients will include labels, music publishers and live businesses, as well as tech start-ups and service companies.

This birds-eye view makes them an invaluable sounding board, and a fantastic network of advice and information. They can be a gateway to new clients, new partners and introductions. They can help you develop a strategy.

Holding a perspective from both sides of the negotiating table, also means your lawyer will have an understanding of how deals can be structured as well as the latest market developments.

How they are compensated for this work will vary, and different lawyers work in different ways.

Some will insist on a percentage commission of deals, while others will charge for their time on an hourly rate (although if your lawyer takes the latter approach, then try to insist that their fee is capped). And most will be willing to negotiate. If they recognise longer-term potential in an artist or a manager, an experienced lawyer might be willing to drop some of their fees in order to build trust and foster a relationship. Similarly, a young and upcoming lawyer, though lacking in experience, might be keen to cut their teeth and take a risk as they go about developing a roster.

The dynamics at the heart of these relationships can be fascinating.

On the one hand, it is typical that legal fees are added to the payment the artist or writer receives when they sign a label or publishing deal. In other words, your client's lawyer is probably getting paid by the party you are in negotiations with – and these companies will evidently provide a substantial part of their cash flow.

However, while this balance of power might appear to favour "the industry", it's also true that managers will provide lawyers with a substantial amount of repeat business.

Similarly, once a deal is agreed, the in-house lawyers at labels and publishers can frequently become useful allies, and a fantastic source of knowledge and guidance.

In other words, there is a considerable degree of fluidity to manager-lawyer relations.

As a rule, the manager should ensure that their hand is on the wheel, and that they are dictating the direction of travel in any negotiations. However, solid legal advice will help inform your decision making and should provide you with greater understanding, clarity and certainty about your chosen course of action.

In short, retaining and engaging the services of a trusted lawyer is worth its weight in gold.

WHAT ARE THE KEY BENEFITS THAT A LAWYER BRINGS TO YOUR TEAM?

"Hire a lawyer and ask them about everything. You only have to do that once, and then you'll know it forever."

Adam Tudhope, Everybody's

"Lawyers offer advice based on solid experience. Some lawyers also bring key networks to you. I believe It's important your lawyer understands different territories especially in a world that's never felt so small, we need someone who can operate in different time zones. This heavily elevates the business."

Nim Jani, Catalyst Management

THE ROLE OF THE MUSIC ACCOUNTANTS

Alongside a lawyer, the other early addition to your team (if you're not using one already) as mentioned in Part One will almost certainly be an accountant – and ideally one who specialises in music-related clients.

If you or your artist have already set up and structured your business as a limited company, then it's likely you'll already be working with a finance professional.

However, if you need to find an accountant then you should seek advice and recommendations – for instance by talking to other managers and MMF members, or by looking through the Music Week directory.

The MMF also has a number of highly regarded accountancy firms as Associate members.

What Do Accountants Do?

At the most basic level, an accountant will ensure that the legal obligations of your company or you as an individual are fulfilled – for instance, that it is registered with HMRC and Companies House, and that your annual tax return is submitted, alongside any personal income tax. In many cases managers may offer business management and bookkeeping, touring in addition.

For most small businesses, this peace of mind alone is often worth paying for.

However, a specialist music accountant can also add substantially to both you and your artist's business – acting as an informal sounding board and a trusted adviser to help you structure a business plan. They will likely help ensure your business is being run efficiently, and take advantage of all the tax planning and expenses to which you might be entitled.

Those accountants with experience of the music business should also understand the intricacies of different sectors, and how money flows into an artist's business from recordings, publishing and live performances.

This can result in invaluable advice to help inform your financial planning.

An accountant can also help structure a manager's commercial relationship with their artist, laying the ground rules for how and when you'll be paid and helping to ensure rules of good governance around that relationship.

If you are planning to partner with another management company, or to work under the umbrella of a larger management company, they can advise on this too.

In other words, relationships with accountants are enormously varied, and based almost entirely on the skill sets that a manager either does or does not possess in-house. For instance, many accountants also offer bookkeeping or business management services to their clients, where they will oversee invoicing, budgeting, cashflows and payments. This is especially true when it comes to an artist's live business, where the volumes of invoices and payments raised might raise cash flow challenges.

However, those managers with less complex business structure might only require the sign-off and submission of end-of-year tax accounts.

Karl Nielson,
Artist Manager

"Having an experienced music accountant on your team is really a fundamental part of managing the business. We all know it's vital that artists have legal expertise when negotiating deals and I have found it equally if not more beneficial to have an accountant look at the numbers that are included in that deal and mock up realistic scenarios and explain to the artists how the words in the contract translate to what they are likely to earn, and what they can expect from statements. The devil is always in the detail and having that early heads up can be extremely illuminating. I also find that artist's really appreciate this when the time comes to consider the offers."

CHAPTER 6

Copyright and Recordings

A s detailed previously, as soon as a song or musical work is composed or recorded, then the copyright owners – both from the underlying composition (the lyrics *and* the music) and the sound recording – have the potential to make money from its exploitation.

As already discussed in Part One, the ownership of sound recordings belongs to the entity that paid for those recordings. Historically, that tended to be a record company, as they exerted control over production, manufacturing and distribution of music.

Under a traditional label contract, the artist would receive an advance (recoupable against their share of revenues and certain other costs) and a pre-agreed royalty rate per album or single sold. They would then sign over their copyrights – usually in perpetuity – and typically for an agreed number of album or track releases.

The artist would then embark on a recording career. The record label would ensure those recordings were distributed to retail and promoted.

This model is now in the process of constant change. Thanks to the dynamics of streaming and social media, the controls around production, manufacturing and distribution of music have dissolved. Subsequently, there has been a power shift

It is now increasingly common for artists to retain ownership of their copyrights – and to either self-release and work directly with a distributor or services company, or to use their leverage to strike a more favourable licensing terms with a label or label services company.

APPROVAL RIGHTS & EQUITABLE REMUNERATION

As detailed in Part One, it is vital that the person or business paying for a recording session (ie the copyright owner of the sound recording) has received approval rights from any session musicians or producers who contributed. This can be done with a standard BPI & MU session agreement which also sets out rates of payment for contributing musicians and PPL Eligible Studio Producer Form.

Agreeing approval rights and registering the musicians and producers involved in the creation of a sound recording also enables public performance revenue to be paid to those contributors whenever that recording is broadcast in public – for instance on the radio or TV.

This is known as "equitable remuneration", commonly abbreviated to ER.

Performers in the UK typically mandate the collection society, PPL, to collect this revenue on their behalf from the various venues and broadcasters. PPL then distributes the income directly to performers and rights owners (e.g. record labels) in accordance with its distribution rules. Importantly, the artist and performer share of this public performance income flows outside of any agreements with record labels.

In other words, this is all incremental revenue – albeit, some sectors of the industry (notably the Musicians Union) have argued strongly that certain "radio-like" elements of on-demand streaming should be subject to rules of ER and flow straight to performers.

Importantly, PPL will also have reciprocal relationships with other international PROs, allowing them to collect and distribute revenue where tracks were played outside of the UK – albeit many other businesses are now moving into this space, and offering to collect what are termed royalties for "neighbouring rights".

How Music Is Licensed
Creating a list of all the different ways that sound recordings can be licensed – and the two different kinds of copyright exploited – would probably result in a book in itself and in fact has done – read the MMF's Dissecting the Digital Dollar to get a

full explanation of licencing practices and how they generate money for artists and songwriters.

Default Copyright Ownership

As previously detailed, in the UK, the owner of the song copyright is the author. Or the "authors" if there are multiple composers involved.

The owner of the recorded right is the entity or individual who organises and pays for the sound recording – which historically, was typically a record label, but increasingly is the artist themselves or a producer.

In both instances, it is absolutely imperative that these ownership splits and allocations are agreed upon at the earliest possible opportunity, and also that this information is uploaded accurately into the relevant music industry databases – in other words with MCPS, PRS and PPL.

For songwriters and artists signed to publishers, labels or label service companies, those businesses will typically take on this type of administrative work. However, where the artist or songwriter is unsigned, or where they administer their own copyrights, then the manager will often be tasked with registering works.

Crucially, copyright owners are able to transfer or "assign" the control and exploitation of their copyrights to other third parties – which is eventually what most artists and songwriters will choose to do, using the experience and assistance of their manager and lawyer to help them navigate the most favourable deal terms and business strategy.

For a manager, this will also likely mean them giving up certain responsibilities and workloads, while adding yet more partners to their client's business for them to ensure they are fulfilling registrations efficiently.

RECORD DEALS

For new artists looking to get their recorded music out into the world there are more choices than ever before, however the competition is also greater and it's much harder to cut through the noise if you're self releasing amongst the 60k other track coming out that day

These considerations can also impact dramatically on the manager's business. For instance, signing with a label might reduce the manager's workload quite significantly – since the label will assume the bulk of responsibilities for releasing and promoting the artist's music. On the flip side, remaining outside of the label system for reasons of creative control, for instance where the artist works with a label services company or sets up their own record label, might leave the manager to do the work, or to devolve the work to other third-party specialists.

There's a lot to weigh up!

But generally, the greater the reliance that the artist has on their label or business partner, then the more control and revenues they are likely to give up. There's now a whole range of other choices too, as already mentioned, which are outlined in some detail in the Deals Guide that was published as part of the MMF's Dissecting The Digital Dollar initiative.

When your artist is ready to start thinking about assigning rights or working with a specialist business partner, these are some of the main things to consider.

Record Labels
As mentioned in Part One, there have been a number of incentives for artists to sign with record labels:

1　A cash advance. As they look to develop a career on multiple fronts, most artists will face cash flow challenges in their early years of development. This is where a label typically steps in – providing an upfront advance that enables the artist to sustain themselves while they make a recording, as well as space to develop their live business or realise their songwriting aspirations. Typically, advances have been recouped from the artist's share of revenues.

2　Creative services. Labels can assume many of the administrative burdens. They will book studios, pair artists with writers and producers, help develop their creative skills, take care of their registrations, develop a coordinated release strategy and offer resources and skills to develop a visual identity, artwork, packaging and other marketing assets required to advance the brands of artists.

3　Physical manufacturing and distribution. As well as overseeing the manufacturing of physical goods like vinyl or CDs, labels will coordinate distribution of products into shops and ensure streaming and download platforms are serviced.

4　Marketing. Labels will help artists grow a fanbase. They will have the budgets, contacts, and infrastructure to maximise opportunities across media, social media, broadcasting and digital. They should also cover the costs of digital and campaign marketing, and potentially the resources to utilise fan data at a global level.

5　Business opportunities. As well as their core services, labels may also be well placed to help artists explore new creative opportunities and new technologies – for instance with areas like gaming, sync licensing, fashion & brand partnerships or NFTs.

6 Royalties & reporting. As detailed by the contract, the label must report back sales, usage and revenues to the artist.

7 Credibility. Having a label onboard and invested in an artist or project will likely increase the interest from other potential partners (e.g. media, retail, brands, others in the industry) and "kitemark" your talent to audiences. As is typical in most businesses, confidence breeds confidence.

In return for these services, the label will negotiate for control of an artist's future recordings.

Most will want an exclusive partnership – either to own an artist's copyrights outright, or to licence them exclusively for a defined period of time or for a defined number of releases.

They will look to agree a share of future revenue with the artist (i.e. a royalty rate) and apply that against the advance they have given or other costs. Most digital royalty rates are upwards of 25% to the artist, although those for physical sales will likely be less and may have certain deductions applied – e.g. for international sales, or packaging, shipment and storage.

The label will also set out how the costs of business will be apportioned. For instance, will these costs be recouped from *all* incoming revenue (i.e. split between artist and label in a "profit share deal") or will they be subtracted only from the artist's share (what's known as a "royalties deal"). While major labels tend to favour royalties deals, so independent labels prefer to go the profit share route and effectively split costs 50/50.

To understand how this differs it's worth considering this example: the artist and label have agreed a 50/50 split, there are £70k in recoupable costs (advance, recording costs etc) and £30k in non-recoupable costs e.g. marketing. So far £250k in income has been generated. On a profit share arrangement, the first £100k would go to cover all costs already incurred, and the next £150k would be split 50/50, so the artist would receive £75k. On a 50% royalties deal (unusually high, normally nearer 25%), half of the money would be allocated to the artist – i.e. £125k – of which £70k would be taken to cover just the recoupable costs paid in advance, not the marketing, so the artist would get £55k.

As already stated, there is no such thing as a "standard record deal", and record labels are having to become increasingly flexible in the types of deals they offer – include "service type" partnerships, where rights are licensed for a fixed period before ownership reverts back to the artist.

WHAT KEY ADVICE WOULD YOU GIVE TO A MANAGER BEFORE THEY NEGOTIATE WITH A RECORD LABEL ON BEHALF OF THEIR ARTIST ?

"Make sure you have more than one label or label services option before you go into serious negotiations as this gives you leverage."

Brian Message, Co Chair, ATC Management

"Before going into negotiation do your homework on the other party. Who have they signed? Does the person you're talking to call the shots or who is their boss? Are they looking after anyone else at the same time? Find out all you can on what their recent deals may have looked like. If you don't get the initial deal offer you want, are there ways you can make it up on the details in the long form?"

Hamish Fingland, Bounse MGMT.

"Get to know the label departments such as international, business affairs, licensing, marketing, brands, touring etc. When you sign with a label, it's the whole shebang that you are working with as a manager, not just the president or the A&R. Knowing which areas of income generation for your client and which department you will rely on will help your negotiation. Labels are far more than advances."

Paul Bonham, Professional Development Director, MMF

Dynamics of the Deal

In a perfect world, your client will be at the epicentre of industry excitement. Radio and media attention will be building, streaming and social media stats rising, fans flocking to live shows and established artists are desperate for an opportunity to collaborate or co-write.

As a result, every record label and music publisher in town will be desperate for their signature, and a bidding war ensues.

And for the lucky few, this is what happens. In a seller's market, the artist, songwriter or producer will have options on the table and in a much stronger position to dictate deal terms. The stars align, the timing is perfect, and they have that thing that every negotiator wants: *leverage*.

Ideally, it means the manager will ensure their client enters into an artist-friendly licensing partnership where they retain full ownership of rights, alongside guarantees of creative control, a large advance, and an equitable share of digital revenues.

In reality, this probably won't be the situation you're blessed with, and it's far more likely that your negotiation experience will involve some horse trading. There'll be some give, and there'll be some take. However, it is still the duty of the manager to secure the best deal possible for their client, and to balance short-term gains with long-term aspirations.

Whilst the artist's lawyer can advise on label negotiations and should be responsible for translating the agreement to legalise in the contract, many managers insist it's their responsibility to lead any negotiations on the deal terms with the label, given their more intimate understanding of the artist's career strategy. They argue this can help secure possible more progressive or innovative terms for the artist than repeating previous agreements or accepting a perceived 'industry standard'. Saying that, a good artist's lawyer should have an understanding of wider label deals and be able to bring this to bear in negotiations.

Some managers perceive the best strategy is to sign with a major label for the biggest advance possible – believing this will ensure their artist remains a priority, even if the individual who signed them leaves the company, simply because of the scale of investment that's been made. Others might see a label or publishing deal as a stepping stone, paving the way to other more lucrative revenue streams such as brand partnerships. Alternatively, you might make a kudos-based decision to partner with a label based on their roster, their catalogue, their ethics or their history.

"Make sure you know the value of the *whole* cherry – a ticket, a stream, a CD, merch etc – in order to establish that none of the middlemen – promoters, agents, record companies, publishers, manufacturers etc, etc – are biting off more than their fair share.

Tim Clark,
Co-founder,
ie:music

As digital technology changes the value of everything so quickly, don't expect all lawyers to keep pace – it is ultimately the manager's responsibility to secure the best deal and to question everything and everybody along the way towards securing it!"

There are a number of divergent factors at play, and, since every negotiation is different, no specific answers – however, MMF members have pointed to some areas that they always prioritise, including:

- Know your client's worth. You should aim to have more than one offer on the table, and be prepared to walk away
- Audit clauses. Make every attempt to futureproof your position, ensuring in writing that any clauses and deal terms can be transparently reviewed. Some managers even push for proof of receipts on costs charged to the artist's account in their audit clause.
- Perpetuity. Over recent years, we've seen most artists and songwriters look to retain long-term ownership of their repertoire, with a preference for licensing deals. However, given the recent number of high-profile catalogue acquisitions, some labels and publishers are now re-seeking a lifetime stake in IP. Managers should be aware of these trends.

TIPS FOR NEGOTIATING A RECORD CONTRACT BY DAVID STOPPS, MANAGER, PROMOTER AND AUTHOR OF BOOK 'HOW TO MAKE A LIVING FROM MUSIC'

"When putting forward a heads of agreement for a recording contract do not start with advances and royalties. Leave those to the end.

This is in order what you should ask for:

1. A licensing agreement and NOT a life of copyright assignment. Make the licence term as short as possible. Start with 15 years. Even if the licence is 50 years it is FAR better than a life of copyright assignment.
2. Artist to receive an income share from record company PPL DUBBING INCOME.
3. Artist to receive a share of record company PUBLIC PERFORMANCE/BROADCASTING income received from non-qualifying countries such as Australia and New Zealand.
4. Advances and royalties etc.

Some artists including artists signed to the majors are receiving income from these sources so make it clear that these income streams are important to you. Push hard for a licensing deal. If you don't ask, you don't get."

- Ensure clarity. Particularly if signing with a smaller label or publisher, make sure you have complete clarity of the roles they'll be performing and paying for (eg digital marketing) and what you'll still be responsible for
- Creative control. The label or publisher representative that you make an agreement with might not stay with the company. A&Rs change jobs. Think about the wider creative culture of your partners, and if your client is likely to retain their long-term support and commitment.
- Build relationships. Ideally, you should get to know staff from all levels, from the label heads to A&R managers and scouts. Aside from good business practice, strategically it means if one leaves then you'll probably be familiar with their replacement.

Artist Services Deals

As mentioned in Part One, for those artists who do not wish to operate within the traditional label system, for instance, by establishing their own label, and plugging into a services type deal with a distributor – the trade offs are pretty clear.

On the upside, they'll retain long-term ownership of their copyrights, and receive a greater cut of revenues when their music is streamed or purchased. They'll also exert greater creative control over how their music is released.

However, creative control usually comes at a cost. Because advances are likely to be smaller, label service or distribution deals will often require the artist to seek alternative sources of investment, and also to outsource at least some of the services traditionally provided by a label – for instance, marketing and promotion.

Such trade offs need to be weighed up, and will almost undoubtedly add costs for the artists and additional workload for their manager.

In this scenario, some managers might look to agree a more flexible fee structure with their client, and charge more for specific services.

Understanding these details and their impacts is all-important when it comes to determining a business plan and negotiating a deal, and there is now a clear trend for artists to pursue partnerships built around an exclusive licence of their copyrights, as opposed to a full assignment of rights in perpetuity.

The length of these licences is also variable, and can be subject to extension, review or buy-out clauses. And obviously, once the term expires, then the rights return to the artist, leaving them free to shop around and seek another deal.

Importantly, artists should also push to insert an auditing clause into their contract, ensuring that an accountant can have access to accounting records and ensuring any discrepancies can be corrected and paid through.

Although more experienced managers might want to negotiate directly with a label or distribution partner on behalf of their client, it is commonplace for the artist lawyer to also be involved and work in tandem to represent the artist's interest.

WHAT DOES YOUR PARTNER PROVIDE?

- ☐ Cash advance
- ☐ Recording costs
- ☐ Artist development
- ☐ Product development
- ☑ Digital distribution
- ☐ Physical manufacture
- ☐ Physical distribution
- ☐ Consumer marketing
- ☐ B2B marketing
- ☐ Press
- ☐ Promotions
- ☐ Social & digital
- ☐ Sync

MUSIC PUBLISHING DEALS

While artists now have greater choice and leverage in how they take their recordings to market, the business of music publishing has been comparably slow in development. In most instances, the machinations of licensing, exploiting and distributing songwriter revenues was devolved completely to music publishers and collection societies.

However, this is no longer the case.

Similar to how the label services model shook up the recording business, a handful of new generation companies – among them, Sentric and SongTrust – have made it more viable for both early stage and established writers to self-manage their song catalogues. This has resulted in increased opportunities for entrepreneurial songwriters and their managers to control and exploit their creativity.

Subsequently, how a songwriter chooses to structure their businesses can have major ramifications on the workload and responsibilities of their manager.

As already detailed in Part One, the controls around song or composition copyright are typically more complex than those around sound recordings – with the latter tending to be "owned" by a single entity, whether that's the featured artist or a record label.

By default, songwriting is more likely to be a collaborative process – with the result that compositions frequently have multiple owners, all potentially working with different business partners.

Although the copyright or "ownership" of a song is inherent from the moment of creation, it is still the responsibility of the writers to establish how that ownership is divided and in what proportions. Similarly, those details also need to be documented and uploaded into the music industry's main databases, such as those belonging to PRS for Music.

Agreeing and apportioning these splits can be a delicate and occasionally contentious process. There might be multiple collaborators involved in the composition of a work, they might not be working in the same physical space (ie they might be composing and sharing ideas online), and, among any group of individuals, some will have more leverage than others. Similarly, in certain genres, the role of the producer, writer and artist is becoming ever more blurred.

The process of determining the size and percentage of splits may be based on any number of factors.

Some bands, for instance, will decide to split songwriting royalties democratically between members. Others will apportion a greater percentage to a single individual or partnership. Equally, where an upcoming artist, writer or producer is collaborating with an established act, they might decide their best long-term interest is to accept a smaller percentage of ownership.

These decisions are determined by leverage, relationships and negotiation. However, it is far better for the manager to push for clarity and agreement at the earliest possible opportunity.

Without these ownership percentages being pre-agreed and without the corresponding metadata being correctly ingested – and whether that job is overseen by a manager, by a traditional music publisher or outsourced to a service company – then there is a strong chance that songwriting royalties will be lost within the system or misallocated.

Making Money From Songs
Because of the structure of rights, and the combination of mechanical and performance rights, the flow of revenues generated from the exploitation of a song are considerably more complex than those generated from a recording.

As outlined in Part One, one of your responsibilities as a manager is to ensure that your client joins a collecting society (most likely PRS for Music in the UK) and starts to register their works.

Performing Royalties
By becoming a PRS member, your client will be assigning control of their performing rights to the collecting society in every song they've written – and every song they'll write or co-write in the future.

Effectively, PRS will own these rights, which they will then offer as part of a collective or blanket licence – offering a combined repertoire of millions of compositions to commercial users (for instance, to a radio station or broadcaster) and negotiating a licence in return.

When a track or composition is broadcast or performed publicly (for instance, on the radio, or performed at a concert) then the monitoring, collection and payment of that revenue is undertaken by PRS – for which they charge the writer an administrative fee. In this way, PRS will, for instance, collect a mandated % of the ticket sales at a gig or festival on behalf of the songwriter, or collect a payment whenever a song is broadcast on the radio or played in a workplace or other commercial setting.

PRS also have reciprocal agreements in place with other collecting societies around the world, which mandates those societies to collect payment for PRS members and forward the revenues (minus *their* administrative fee) for distribution.

These performance royalties are paid directly to the writer, regardless of any contractual agreements, so they can be an incredibly valuable source of revenue.

Consequently, it is important that the manager – or another designated business partner – ensures not only the information about these rights is registered correctly, but also that they are correctly administered and distributed accurately.

Mechanical Royalties
The other rights inherent to the song or composition, are the so-called mechanical right to "reproduce" or make copies and distribute (for instance, in the manufacturing of a CD or vinyl album, or with a digital download or a stream). Complicating matters somewhat, industry convention has dictated that digital downloads and streams exploit both the performing and the mechanical copyright inherent in a song

Historically, writers have monetized these specific rights by either joining MCPS directly – or, more commonly, by assigning them to a music publisher.

To collect mechanical royalties, it is essential that ISRC codes relevant to a specific release are attached to the song data.

Synchronisation Royalties
Beyond performance and mechanical royalties, the other key revenue generated from songs is from synchronisation (or sync) usage – where a song is placed under a visual image (eg a game, advert or in a movie soundtrack) and a fee is negotiated.

Any sync usage has to be agreed by owners of both the master recording (ie the artist, producer or label) and the song owners – with the fee generally split 50/50.

The role of a Publisher
As with record labels, there can be a number of potential benefits to your client signing with a music publisher, including:

- Investment: Publishers will generally pay a lump sum cash advance to a writer, which will be pegged against future royalty earnings.

- Creative support: Increasingly, managers are closely involved in the A&R process, but good publishers will also be adept at helping writers develop their craft and find creative collaborators – whether that's a network of other artists or writers to work with, or potential commercial opportunities with advertising agencies, TV production companies or games developers.

- Commercial support: As above, a good music publisher will have well established networks. They will have contacts, and should be incentivised to proactively look for commercial opportunities. Unlike the collecting societies' blanket licensing of performance rights, the biggest publishers will look to agree direct deals with the largest digital music services – which they claim will result in better terms for their writers.

- Efficiencies: Where royalties are generated overseas, an established music publisher will likely be a member of the local collecting society and can therefore receive royalties directly – rather than see them flow from the local collecting society to the collecting society of the writer. As well as ensuring greater accuracy, this can greatly speed up the distribution and payment of royalties.

- Administrative support: Publishers are also data businesses. They should shoulder the work of ensuring songwriter data is accurately uploaded onto the correct databases, that usage is monitored, that data conflicts are resolved, and that revenues are flowing efficiently. The bigger publishers also operate as global businesses. They will be members of the major collecting societies, and operate in other major markets – either directly or by outsourcing to a sub-publisher.

As with record labels and artists, the terms of an agreement between a writer and a music publisher are negotiable – and similar to a record contract, the basic principle still applies that there is push and pull between the creator ceding certain controls and ownership rights in return for revenues, support and services.

How much control and ownership is ceded (and how much finance is received) will, of course, be determined by the perceived talent of the composer and the perceived value of their songs.

A writer or producer with an established track record of writing "hits" will be able to exert greater leverage than an individual with unproven talent.

Similarly, there may be positives and negatives to signing with a major or independent. For instance, the former will have larger budgets and global networks, but there is also a risk that your writer may not be perceived as a priority. An independent might pay a small advance, but offer specialist services or credibility in a certain genre that a major cannot match.

As always, these decisions should tally with short term and long term aspirations of your client.

And although every publishing deal will be slightly different, some standard principles generally apply across the industry.

1 Publishers do not control performance rights – however they do usually take a share of performance royalties. As before, performance rights are generally assigned directly by the writer to a collecting society like PRS for Music. The society then controls (and effectively owns) these rights.

However, in a typical publishing deal, a music publisher will negotiate to receive a share of the writer's performance royalties. In practice, this means that a collecting society like PRS for Music will split the writer's share and pay a portion of it directly to the publisher.

2 Mechanical rights work differently. A music publisher might strike a direct licensing agreement with a digital music service – or they might licence the service via MCPS. If it's the former, then the music service pays the publisher directly. If it's the latter, then MCPS pays the publisher, who then pays the writer.

For physical products like vinyl or CDs, it is the responsibility of the recording rights holder (e.g. a record label) to apply for an MCPS licence and pay through the writer's share. In the UK, that generally means 8.5% of the dealer price (i.e. the price paid to the retailer) is allocated for song royalties. By comparison about 12-15% of total digital streaming revenues are paid through publishing rights combined mechanical and performance via PRS and your publisher.

3 Publishing contracts tend to be shorter than recording contracts. In a modern music publishing contract, you would expect rights to be assigned for a fixed period of time and to cover a specific number of compositions. Publishing deals can be as short as 10-15 years and in perpetuity deals are rare and often looked down upon as the long term value and exploitation of the songs then rests with the punisher not the writer.

4 Deal terms tend to favour the writer. Generally, mechanical rights will be allocated in the writer's favour in a ratio of 80/20 or 70/30, while performance royalties are frequently split 50/50. In other words, a collecting society like PRS for Music will typically distribute half a song's performance earnings direct to the writer, and the other half direct to their publisher. The fact that royalty agreements are weighed in the writer's favour means that publishing advances often retain less importance than recording advances – by virtue that publishing advances are far more likely to recoup.

As highlighted at the start of this chapter, a traditional music publishing deal is not the only option available for writers.

**Nick Myers,
co-founder,
Fast Friends**

WHAT ARE THE BENEFITS OF SIGNING WITH A PUBLISHER?

"In my experience, it really depends on the team you sign with and how engaged they are with the writer following signing, this is more important than the name on the door or global footprint of the company. We encourage our clients only to sign with a publisher that has relationships relevant to their needs, will be proactive enough to use them, and commands the respect and/or has the leverage to bring opportunities to them that we as management aren't able to otherwise. When that goes well, a writer's success and fortunes can accelerate rapidly.

But it's not easy to find the right person or team that actually are going to bat for your writer and keep the heat on once the deal is done and they are onto their next signing target. For that reason, we don't chase publishing deals and in most cases, it might take a few years before publishers start reaching out to us, and even longer before one of our writers signs their first deal following a lot of publisher 'dating'.

In the meantime, as with most writer managers, we are acting as their de-facto publisher, sourcing co-writing opportunities for them, levelling them up into rooms with more experienced writers and higher-profile artists. During this time, we frequently sign our writers up with publishing services companies like SongTrust so that their mechanicals and publisher performance royalties are being collected globally and efficiently. There's no creative input from these companies, but they do what they do very well and we feel it's a no brainer when their terms allow you to pull your writers / their catalogues out of their administration at relatively short notice should you need to, once that right publishing deal comes along."

Increasingly, we are seeing MMF members work outside this system and helping their clients to self-publish and operate their own music publishing operation, or to agree "administration" or "co-publishing" agreements.

Sandy Dworniak, founder of This Much Talent

"I have deals with both major and indie publishers and in my experience it varies a lot from company to company. Some do lots, some do nothing, regardless of their size. With a major it's often about the advance but for me it's much much more about the A&R person and the team over all. I always look for a situation that is proactive on behalf of the writer, both in putting them in key sessions but also pushing on sync. We have two admin deals and they actually care about the clients career and are proactive, as opposed to just simply collecting income. We've made money as a result of dining with them. With regards to the service companies they did absolutely nothing for my client – so it was a total waste of time compared to other company admin deals with advances!"

Similar to employing a label services company for recorded rights, such decisions will undoubtedly have implications on the workload of a manager and there may be an expectation that you will fulfil or outsource the roles – and possibly pursue the finance – otherwise provided by a music publisher.

There are a number of service or "song management" companies that offer to take on the administrative burden of music publishing – registering a songwriter's works with societies all around the world, as well as tracking usage and collecting royalties.

By registering songs directly with multiple societies, these companies will also chase down overseas performance royalties and, in theory, provide greater efficiencies than using the collecting societies reciprocal system.

As with the label services model for recordings, songwriters retain ownership of rights under this model and are charged a small admin fee. Some of these companies will also offer additional services, such as synchronisation expertise – although a manager might also bring in a third-party specialist.

Some music publishers will also offer similar administrative deals. As above, under these partnerships, the songwriter retains ownership of their rights and contracts the publisher to handle their business (e.g. registrations, tracking, reporting, distribution) for a specified time period.

SONG ROYALTY CHAINS

One of the major challenges facing writers and their managers in terms of streaming royalties is the issue of so-called "royalty chains".

As detailed in the MMF's $ong Royalties Guide, this is where reciprocal agreements between international collecting societies, publishers, sub-publishers and the largest digital music service become so complex and convoluted that flows of songwriting revenues are being mismatched, misallocated or snarled up in ownership disputes.

As a result, while it can take months for an artist to receive royalties after their recordings were streamed (if they are on a direct distribution deal), for a songwriter it might take several years before they receive payment.

Because of inefficiencies in the global distribution infrastructure, it means songwriters are at risk of losing valuable songwriting income – especially if they do not have a manager or other appointed representative ensuring registrations have been submitted correctly and accurately.

CHAPTER 7

Direct to Fan Revenues

A s covered in Section One, these days most D2F businesses are informed by data, the ability to locate your audience and to use this information to develop a business strategy, and to communicate details of new releases or upcoming gigs is commonplace for almost every artist. As well as this kind of targeted communication, data can also help an artist to profile their audience (e.g. their age, location, tastes) and to test a campaign to see what resonates.

However, when an artist starts working with a range of different business partners, and begins accumulating and cross-referencing data from a multitude of different sources, this is when things can get really interesting. Streaming data, for instance, which might reveal the location of an artist's most fervent fans, might help with planning of a live tour. Similarly, data from ticket sales, might help inform an album release campaign

Typically it will be the manager's responsibility to liaise with their artist's partners to agree advance access to any data they control, and to ensure its collection is compliant with General Data Protection Legislation (GDPR) rules.

MMF FAN DATA GUIDE

Published in 2019 as part of the MMF's Dissecting The Digital Dollar initiative, the Fan Data Guide illustrates in some detail ten different kinds of data sources available to artists, as well as information on how to access this data, its ownership, and key questions for managers to ask business partners when negotiating a deal.

These 10 different data sources are:

- Email data
- Website data
- Social data
- Streaming data
- Ticketing data
- Advertising data
- Smark-Link data
- Affiliate-Link data
- Re-marketing data
- D2F Store data

Some of these data sources should be directly accessible to the artist and their manager (e.g. through social media channels) while others (e.g., for instance, details of ticket purchasers) will be controlled by business partners .

However, as the guide highlights:

"Managers feel that – because the fan relationship ultimately belongs to the artist, not to the platforms they use or the business partners they work with – as much of this data as possible should be shared with the artist and their management team. Indeed, given the fan's relationship is usually with the artist, not the business partners, they too would prefer that artists first and foremost have access to this information.

"So, while it may well be that an artist's business partners make more use of some or all of this data on a day-to-day basis, artists should nevertheless be able to access all this information to inform their businesses, and should be assured that they won't lose any data or access to any data if and when they move business partners."

Certainly, most managers would push for contracts to include clauses that allow their artist access and ownership over as much of their data as possible, and, where possible, to ensure all online accounts (eg for their website, MailChimp, Facebook, Twitter, Snap, Discord, Twitch and so on) are registered in the artist's name.

In other words, the optimum position is that the artist owns the keys, with access being granted to partners when appropriate.

For instance, for Facebook/Instagram, the artist can set up a Meta Business Manager account and then give third parties (e.g. a label, brand or promoter) permissions to access and run advertising when appropriate.

As well as clarifying permissions and controls, successful online marketing also requires a budget. And while, in the early stages of their career, your artist is likely to be using their own resources for asset creation (eg making short-form videos) and spending their own money on social media advertising, much of this activity will likely be assumed by labels, distributors, retailers, brands, promoters and ticket companies as their career progresses, with an expectation that the artist will support in order to boost commercial activity.

As highlighted by the MMF's Managing Expectations report, however, some more established management companies are employing digital specialists in-house, helping their clients retain greater control over how they are marketed online. With so many competing demands for new and interesting content to feed social media platforms, this can also alleviate some of the increased marketing demands being placed on artists. Concerns about these demands, and the pressure to be "always on", is leading to a greater acknowledgement of the need to safeguard artists from "digital burnout".

The MMF has been at the heart of this discussion, publishing a well-received report on Digital Burnout in May 2022. This also included a series of recommendations, including wider recognition of the need for greater artist support - for instance, providing budget and expertise for content creation, agreeing a specified "time out" for artists away from social media, and also providing more meaningful information about the tangible impacts of digital marketing campaigns.

BRAND PARTNERSHIPS

Most managers think that branding deals and opportunities are only for big superstar acts, but there are also many branding deals to be had for brand new, buzz and mid level acts too. Brand partnerships for an artist at any level can be a fantastic additional stream of income and in many cases, an important life line.

Plus if done strategically in alignment with other activities such as a new track on tastemaker streaming playlists, getting spins on radio, club plays, PR campaigns and live dates, a branding deal can not only fund your act, but it can also be a component in a springboard to help propel an artist to more attractive licensing, publishing or record deal options.

"As a new manager, I fell into brand partnerships with a new hotly tipped independent artist who ended up having a whole commercial release campaign funded by a major global fashion brand. I found this kind of deal was as lucrative as the recording deals on the table, while also allowing us to own the masters. Plus we didn't have to recoup any expenditure. So I decided to revise my management strategy /business plan, choosing to work with artists that wanted the same types of opportunities, were brand-partnership-friendly and as artists, also commercially appealing. I decided to dedicate a good portion of my time and energy going after and securing brand partnership deals as hard as I went after recording/publishing/licensing and sync deals."

Anneliese Harmon, Music Exec, Entrepreneur and GM at MMF

Brand partnership deals are not for every artist. Some want to focus solely on their music so it's important to discuss and fully understand what your artist is comfortable with.

People often ask what is the best way to secure brand partnership deals. Like most deals for an artist, many partnership deals come via contacts new and old, of a manager or management team. These contacts are a result of years of hard work, constant networking, relationship building, referrals, introductions, industry events and non stop updating, pitching, exploring and suggesting options to connect dots of new opportunity.

There are also some branding companies that act as brokers and agencies who are well embedded, with inside contacts at brands and in communication and advertising agencies. They may also approach artists and their managers directly or have an existing relationship that is amped up when the right offer comes up. However it's important to note that these companies are in businesses to connect and facilitate, and don't have a long-term strategy with the artist. It's a transaction and as such, they will take a considerable cut straight off the top before payment event makes it to the artist for other normal deductions and splits.

Some record labels have their own full time in-house branding departments that are focused on creating, building and maintaining long-term relationships with brands and agencies, in order to get in briefs regularity and in volume, directly at source. Labels may also get many brand partnership opportunity briefs coming in for their top superstar artists, that are often turned down, but then can be shared and offered to other artists on the label.

However with the popularity of 360 deals for artists in exchange for higher advances, no matter who brings in the deal, managers must accept, if a 360 deal has been agreed, and the artist is un-recouped, regardless who found the brand deal, the artist still may never see this income.

Still the pros of brand partnerships are many and do outweigh the cons. Branding deals are often specific to a region, leaving open many options to seek out work with the same brands in other countries.

Also, it's important to note that what may be considered high risk and a lot of money to invest for a label or publisher, is sometimes not considered as much of a risk or as expensive to a brand. As a result, funds earned in a brand deal campaign can provide significant support to a new or independent artist's career. Through brand partnerships, a manager can secure solid financing to pay for an artist's recording, legal fees, photos shoots, social media marketing, videos, press/radio/playlist plugging and live show shortfall and more.

And the best thing of all? Unlike label/publishing deals with advances, brand deal payment and future income is normally non-recoupable. If independent, the artist can get income and can still maintain exclusive ownership rights for their masters and songs.

In addition the marketing support around a successful brand partnership activation will increase the visibility and profile of an artist on social media and in real life, which if planned properly, can create solid growth momentum making the artist and their own brand project more appealing to labels, publishers and other potentially more lucrative brand partners.

Branding deals also sometimes allow independent artists and their manager the breathing space needed to make the right deals at the right time and avoid positions of financial desperation or debt. With lucrative branding deals, artists can pay for living and business expenses without borrowing from a label or publisher.

"The essential thing is to understand the new business models available to make alternative income for your artists. There are multiple industries within the music industry, so don't be afraid to explore and try new platforms. The phrase 'If you want something you've never had, you've got to do something you've never done' comes to mind."

Des Agyekumhene, Music Manager and Entrepreneur

Top New & Mid Level Artist Branding Tips

- Many brands like working with credible 'buzz' artists with growth potential. They look at these as early investments and long term relationships that can flourish and grow over time.

- Make sure the brand deal represents the artist, their vision and their future. A brand deal can damage an artist and the brand if not coming from an authentic place. No deal is worth losing credibility, so the artist must truly believe in the brand and not just be looking for a cheque.

- Make sure the deal pays a fair price for activation and is for an agreed set term with clearly defined deliverables. This is especially crucial with new brands who may not know exactly what they expect yet.

- Work with a legal representative on the contract and build those costs into the bottom line of what you need financially to seal the deal.

- Pay attention to brand deal exclusivity, term and value. Signing a global exclusive deal for a long time may seem like a big win at the time, but may not be over time if the artist has a major hit or loses out on potentially bigger deals and opportunities in the future further down the line.

- Remember short term deals with options to renegotiate are the best with brands. If it's going really well you can adjust and increase payment terms. Either way, to continue, the brand will need to pay you again.

- Know your artists' worth, their audience, appeal and what they are bringing.

- Cash is king and always will be. Free things are great, but should be seen as a bolt on perk, not a substitute for payment. You can't pay your bills with them.

- Do good work, deliver what you agreed and if a term ends and isn't renewed, part on good terms. The community is small, and you never know where those on a brand's teams will end up next and where that could lead.

- Network and build relationships with brands as strongly as with the music industry. Many deals are placed though connections and don't even make it out of the building or on to the open market.

PROMOTION: PRESS, PR & PLUGGING

Another area where your artist will require additional support and expertise is with promotion, which will typically mean employing a press agency as well as specialised plugging services.

Although record labels will provide in-house promotional services, artists will often choose to work with an outside agency that specialises in a particular genre or area. These companies will either be paid on a retainer (i.e. a fixed sum each month) or on a project-by-project basis, and will typically cover one specific area of the media. For example, you might have to employ multiple agencies to cover national, regional and online, or to assist with social media support.

You would expect a PR company to have a good range of contacts in their chosen field, and the capability to produce a compelling media strategy that compliments your commercial strategy. Essentially they will be amplifying and communicating your artist's activities – for instance, writing press releases to announce record releases or live shows, arranging interviews and photo shoots, or pitching for reviews - although a PR representative would also be expected to field incoming enquiries from journalists.

Some PR's will also offer media training, and should help your artist connect with supportive journalists who – hopefully – become champions of their music. As well as generating media activity, PR's will also collate and provide reports of any coverage – all of which can be useful to provide to labels, DSPs and live bookers, showing evidence of interest and credibility in your artists, and adding to their career momentum.

Finding a press agent is usually done through word of mouth. If you are an MMF member you can ask other managers for their recommendations on the MMF Facebook group. The Music Week directory also offers a comprehensive list of those operating in the UK.

Similarly, beyond the promotion expertise offered by labels and other recording partners, many artists will choose to work with independent pluggers who will pitch for inclusion on national and regional radio, as well as for TV.

Pluggers play a vital role in career development and most managers will develop strong relationships with a certain plugger valuing their input into processes such as A&R for radio edits and helping build long term relationships with stations for their clients.

CHAPTER 8

Beginning to Tour

MANAGEMENT COMMISSION

As we highlighted in Part One, for the majority of artists, and therefore, for the majority of artist managers, live music is their primary source of revenue. As your artists audience grows so does their earnings from the live business (although their costs often increase as well)

In most cases, this revenue is paid as commission against their client's net earnings from performing at live shows. However, if you scratch beneath the surface, there is a lot of variation in how different managers operate.

For instance, while it's commonplace for managers to commission 20% net of their client's live income, others will commission on gross earnings – or a combination of gross and net.

Similarly, there are also managers who take a more tailored approach, and segment their client's performances into different categories and charge accordingly – i.e. they'll commission different rates for headline appearances and support slots, festivals, DJ sets or personal appearances.

These approaches will often depend on the service that the manager provides, the range of activities they're involved with, and the genre their artist operates within. There are no hard and fast rules.

However, given that live revenue might make or break your management business, it is essential to have a viable agreement in place with your artist. From the outset, you do not want to be in a position where everyone else in the team (e.g. the booking agent, tour manager, accountant) is being paid upfront or a set guaranteed fee, while you as the manager have no certainty of being paid at all.

Live music represents the most labour intensive part of the business and, as a manager, the multitude of planning, budgeting and logistical tasks can potentially eat up a significant amount of time.

Against this, the revenues from live music can be unpredictable, while the costs to put on and promote a show are very often immovable.

BUILDING A LIVE TEAM

For all of these reasons, as soon as your artist starts to gain traction and perform beyond their local region, and as soon as a semblance of complexity enters their touring plans, it makes sense for them to outsource some specific responsibilities.

As a result of this outsourcing and through this expansion of the live team, the role that you play will shift accordingly.

But before we explore those changes, who are these people likely to join your team? What role do they play? And how are they paid?

Booking Agent

A good booking agent will help an artist build their live career. They will negotiate with promoters and festival organisers to secure live appearances and find opportunities. Working alongside the manager, they establish ticket prices and fees, and help the artist plan and execute touring campaigns. Most agents will look to partner with an artist at an early stage of their career, and help them develop.

The best agents will have a wide range of contacts with event organisers and festival bookers, and can really help an artist push their live career forward.

The biggest four agencies (CAA, Wasserman, WME, UTA) are huge global businesses that represent a range of entertainment clients. However, there are also scores of independent and genre-specialist agencies too. For their services, agents are typically paid 10% of the artist's gross earnings for a show.

Promoter

The promoter pays for the show to take place. They book the venue, and work with agents and managers to create, budget, market and sell the event. Some promoters (e.g. Live Nation, AEG Presents) are global in scale, while many others are independent with strong regional or genre expertise.

In practice, artists are contracted by the promoter to deliver a show to a set of agreed specifications – and then paid according to the terms of that contract in a final "settlement".

As previously mentioned in Part One the settlement might be structured around a "guarantee" (i.e. a pre-agreed lump sum, minus certain expenses) or on the basis of ticket sales – or a combination of a guarantee *and* ticket sales. Although some artists will work exclusively with a single promoter, it is also common practice to use multiple promoters – or even for two or more promoters to partner on a single event.

Tour Manager

This is the manager's person on the ground. They are expected to accompany the artist on tour, and take responsibility for ensuring day-to-day logistics go to plan – for instance, with travel, accommodation, finances and budgets. Typically paid a daily rate, a good tour manager can provide the glue between artist, manager, crew, agent, promoter, and venue.

In practice, the tour manager will usually be responsible for pre-production and advancing information with venues and promoters and be expected to create a day sheet that provides details of each day's schedule – ensuring that artists and crew know where they need to be and when. Crucially, they will also manage the tour's finances, overseeing expenditure on the road and ensuring that incomings/outgoings are kept within the agreed touring budget. They will also help fix problems as they arise (promoter disputes, lost passports, guest list requests) and may even take on additional duties, such as driving or working the merchandise stand.

Production Manager/Road Crew

For larger shows, a production manager, assisted by a road crew ("roadies") is likely to work alongside the tour manager to ensure all technical elements are in place – whether that's the load in/load out, setting up of instruments and equipment, lighting, sound, soundchecks, and basic health and safety.

How an artist and manager outsource responsibilities to these different roles will ultimately depend on the type and complexity of shows they wish to perform. Many artists will utilise the expertise of all these individuals in their team; whereas, for others, the manager might take on the role of booking agent (or vice versa!) or tour manager.

Live music relationships

○ **ARTIST COMMUNICATES WITH MANAGER**
What type of shows do they want to perform, how do these shows align with their marketing / promotional plans and long-term goals

○ **ARTIST AND MANAGER LIAISE WITH BOOKING AGENT**
Artist team discuss opportunities and potential bookings

○ **MANAGER, BOOKING AGENT AND ACCOUNTANT LIAISE WITH PROMOTERS**
Artist team meets promoter to nail down touring plans, agree budgets and logistics (eg hiring musicians, paying for equipment / stage set)

○ **PROMOTER ORGANISES SHOW, AGREES CONTRACT WITH ARTIST TEAM**
Artist agrees terms with promoter, contract reviewed by manager and lawyer

○ **PROMOTER, VENUE, TICKET COMPANY & ARTIST TEAM ANNOUNCE, PROMOTE AND MARKET SHOW**
Artist announces touring plans through their socials and press release to media. Promoters, venues and ticketing agents market the shows through a combination of digital promotion and advertising.

○ **ARTIST PERFORMS SHOW**
Artist performs as per the terms of their contract, and tour manager agrees the "settlement" (ie payment – agreed revenues minus agreed costs).

○ **PAYMENT**
Settlement is paid directly to the agent's bank account, and then forwarded to the artist less commission. Tour manager, manager and other service providers invoice for payment.

SHOW PLANNING

Establishing your artist's worth on the live circuit, and securing the venues and shows they want to play will be determined by a range of factors – some of which will be beyond your control. However, the price of their tickets and size of their guarantee will ultimately be decided through a conversation between management, booking agent and promoter, before being agreed in a contractual agreement.

At this advance stage, you will need to make clear to your artist what is expected of them in terms of performance – as well as providing them with information of expected payment, as well as their "technical rider" (ie details of the the PA, lights, stage planning and production), and "hospitality rider" (catering, accommodation, transport and guestlist requirements).

Any costs and outlays not agreed in advance are liable to be deducted from the artist's settlement.

These details will eventually be bound up in the artist-promoter contract, as well as specified in the "advance sheet" which lays out key information of show logistics – e.g. details and specifications of venues, times of load-in and load-out, stage set up, etc.

Ideally, this process of planning and consultation can help inform a longer-term conversation about the size and expense of show production your artist can aspire to, as well as the kinds of venues and events their career trajectory might lead towards.

Success is always relative. Not every artist is suited to headlining the biggest arenas and festivals – and in fact, the vast majority won't be. However, most artists will hold an aspiration of where they would like to end up, whether that's performing at a specific venue or in a certain market.

The aim for most artists is to grow and evolve; to build an audience over time, to retain that audience, and to satisfy their creative and commercial goals.

LIVE CONTRACTS

The contract between a promoter and an artist will typically be issued by your agent, and detail the following:

Logistics: Basic information about the venue, the date/time the artist is expected to perform, and the duration of the performance.

Kerry Harvey-Piper, Red Grape Music

"Working with grassroots independent artists the team is often small. In addition to being the manager I might also be their label, their booking agent or their tour manager on occasion wearing all 4 hats at once. My income comes either from 20% of artist income, or an hourly consultancy rate depending. If I'm the TM, I additionally charge the artist an on-the-road day rate. It's not as straightforward as it could be, but I identify and time-track every task (www.Toggl.com is brilliant for this).

In 2020 I booked a 43 date UK tour for an artist, around two thirds booked direct with venues (e.g. arts centres) and the rest with local promoters. Budget-wise, it was important for this tour to break even across the whole tour on fees alone. With a touring party of 4 (2 musicians, a sound engineer and me as TM) in a self-drive hired transit van. Pre-tour, I did all the contracting, show advancing, hotel booking & all logistics as this artist has very specific needs (elderly and classed as disabled) which could have been overlooked if I'd contracted the work out. I've dealt with similar situations where an artist was touring with a baby and it's vital to ensure that the artists' individual needs are going to be understood by the venues & hotels.

At this level, everyone in the touring party has to be multiskilled and be able to multitask on the road. Shit happens of course but a hands-on approach and a positive attitude goes 99% of the way to solving most things. 7650 miles and over 6000 ticket sales later, the tour made a profit both on gig fees and on merch, 75% of the venues sold out AND everyone's been properly paid. Running things like this is exhausting, stressful and all-consuming, but watching the show come together, hearing the live performances and seeing the audiences clearly having a great time is one of the biggest satisfactions of my job."

Payment terms: e.g. for a headline show, an artist might be contracted to receive a guaranteed sum or 85% of net box office receipts – whichever is greater. For a festival appearance, they might receive a specific guaranteed sum. Payment will often be split 50% ahead of performance, and 50% post-performance – with the money transferred directly to the agent. The promoter will typically be contracted to bear responsibility for any local taxation considerations and collecting society levies. You may wish to specify late payment terms as we are hearing post-COVID that show settlements are now slipping as late as a month after the show due to ticket no-shows and staffing issues at venues. This can cause major issues for an artist's cash flow.

Ticket price: The contract will usually stipulate that ticket prices or fees cannot be changed without permission from the artist, and that tickets will not be placed onto the secondary market i.e. on ticket resale websites like viagogo or StubHub. (Artists wishing to minimise online ticket touting can find more information at www. fanfairalliance.org.) The promoter is also usually obliged to provide a regular sales update.

Allocation of costs: What else is the promoter responsible for? Will they also be providing transport, accommodation, PA, lights and catering? Will they be providing a rider? How many guest passes will the artist receive? Will the promoter be obligated to provide documentation or invoices for venue rental, advertising costs etc? All this detail should be in the contract.

Creative: Many contracts will stipulate that the artist's image or artwork cannot be misappropriated, or to be used by third-party sponsors (e.g. brands) without permission. Similarly, the artist is not under obligation to partake in interviews or promotion.

Marketing: The contract might include a guarantee of marketing and promotional spend by the promoter.

Merchandise: Making clear that the artist has the exclusive right to sell merchandise at the show. See section below on Merch which outlines issues with venue commissions that you may wish to try to tackle in the contract.

Licensing: Making clear that no recording of the performance should be made available without the artist's permission. This clause is increasingly relevant for festivals, which are now frequently live streamed or recorded for broadcast.

Data: Artists are increasingly insisting that the promoter provide a contact database of ticket purchasers, subject to GDPR legislation.

Environmental concerns: In order to allay concerns about the environmental impact of touring, many artists are adding specific "green" clauses to their contracts, for instance banning the use of single-use plastics. See the section on Climate Action below for more information.

Liability: Most contracts will include a clause absolving the artist or touring party from any liability resulting from the actions of customers attending the performance, including any damage sustained to the venue.

Insurance: Additionally, there should also be a clause demanding the promoter has secured employer's liability insurance and public liability insurance to cover the artist's personal property and equipment, as well as damage to the venue or claims made by customers or staff.

Cancellation: Importantly, a contract should detail what happens if a show is cancelled – and who is liable for compensation should the other party be at fault. All contracts should also include a so-called "force majeure" clause – which effectively terminates the contract and renders it void if a show is cancelled due to an "Act of God".

FINANCING A TOUR

Once your artist is capable of selling "hard tickets" (i.e. performing shows where they are the headliner or main attraction) they will inevitably attract interest from promoters. As mentioned above, as a headliner on your own tour your artist is likely now to be on both a minimum guarantee negotiated by your booking agent (circa >£100-250 for a 200 cap venue depending on the size of a crowd you can draw, or >£500 for a 500 cap venue), plus an 80/20 share of ticket revenue beyond a break even point for the promoter (which could be around 50% of tickets sold).

However, even with money coming in as already outlined, touring can be expensive and productions can be cost-heavy. There can be alot of parties to be invoiced, and payment demands can be fast and furious.

Live music also depends on economics of scale. For a tour to be profitable, the outgoing costs of production are just as important as any incoming ticket and merchandise revenue.

Equally, depending on the size and scale of your artist's operation and the number of people involved, your artist might need to draw audiences of several thousand people before their live business gains traction.

Consequently, artists will frequently look to their manager and their wider team to secure additional sources of revenue to help sustain their touring activity, or to help them make efficiencies and savings.

When planning the routing of a tour, it's almost inevitable that some performances will end up subsidising others. Playing a full-capacity hometown show, for instance, might free up the budget to explore previously untapped regional or international markets. Similarly, a manager might organise a small number of regional shows, creating opportunities to sell tickets and merchandise, to subsidise a less lucrative but promotionally rewarding mid-afternoon slot at a festival. This is why planning is so important.

There are innumerable ways in which your artist can raise additional finance for touring, but some of the more obvious avenues to explore include:

Tour support from a record label

Historically, record labels have helped subsidise the cost of touring as part of their marketing remit – providing finance to help support their contracted artists to perform in front of an audience, and, with a bit of luck, opening up promotional opportunities to help drive vinyl or CD sales. Such "tour support" was almost always recoupable from the artist's royalties, albeit it also enabled them to keep loss-making shows on the road and build up their live business.

This situation remained commonplace into the early 2000s, when there was a trend for 360-deals and cash-strapped labels sought to negotiate a slice of an artist's live or merch revenues. And in today's streaming era, tour support is still commonly available – albeit at reduced levels. 360 deals are still an option.

Predictably, an artist will typically need to be signed to a major or larger indie in order to access this kind of funding. They will also be expected to supply their label with a detailed budget, showing the cost and benefits breakdown of their proposed touring schedule.

Industry and Commercial Funding:

There are several industry grants available to fund live music activity, the most prominent being the PPL Momentum Music Fund which is administered by PRS Foundation. Established in 2013, and aimed at artists who can provide evidence of current career success, Momentum offers funding of up to £15,000 to help support touring, recording or marketing projects. Importantly, since they are often the person filling in the application form, Momentum allows for managers to include a "project contribution budget line" to pay for their time and expertise.

Another hugely important fund is Music Export Growth Scheme (MEGS), a joint initiative between the UK Government and the UK recorded music industry (the scheme is managed by the BPI) that make available grants ranging from £5,000 – £50,000 to UK-registered independent music companies to assist them with marketing campaigns when looking to introduce successful UK music projects overseas. To be eligible, applicants must be a UK-based music company with a turnover of less than €50 million and fewer than 250 employees.

Help Musicians also offer a smaller Touring & Live Support fund of up to £5,000, which also includes tailored sessions of business and health advice, while other schemes place a focus on overseas activity – notably the PRS Foundation's International Showcase Fund, which helps artists travel to high profile showcasing events such as SXSW.

For overseas showcases, and particularly for SXSW which can be ferociously expensive, a manager would be advised to undertake a significant amount of planning and preparation – ensuring that meetings and other activities are lined up in advance.

Other potential funding opportunities can be found from third-party brand sponsors. These partnerships are typically confined to the biggest artists performing on the biggest stages, but some entrepreneurial managers have found ways to incorporate commercial brand deals into their artist's live business.

FUNDING TIPS FROM JOE FRANKLAND AT PRS FOUNDATION

With a plethora of opportunities managers can apply for on behalf of their clients, plus direct support available through the MMF Accelerator programme, POWER UP, Keychange and other open calls, there have never been as many ways to access grant funding in the UK. However, there's also record levels of demand and the world of funding can be confusing and frustrating. I hope these tips help to demystify the process and provide food for thought so you can focus efforts in the right areas and increase your chances of success.

1 Do some research first

Invest time in exploring the different types of support on offer. Take advantage of funding wizards, guidance pages, advice videos and conference panels. And talk to other managers and creators who have successfully applied for funding.

I understand it can be daunting and we're all very busy, but few things are as frustrating as listening to incredible music submitted by an applicant, only to realise they're applying to the wrong fund, asking for the wrong things, or submitting plans for activity that happens before funding decisions are made.

Funders are generally very approachable so don't be afraid to reach out, ask questions and get to a point where you're applying to fewer open calls because you've picked the right funding scheme at the right time.

2 Keep it simple and make yourself clear

Chances are the person listening to and reading your application has a limited amount of time to get through 20-50 applications. Assuming the music you're submitting is outstanding, your task becomes about ensuring the application lives up to the same standards and jumps out.

Many funders use external advisors which means there is an industry expert and music fan on the other side of the process. Instead of getting caught up in complex language and jargon, be clear, concise and use direct language. If in doubt, think about how you would outline plans to a fellow industry professional.

3 Show the impact funding will have

By the end of the application, funders and external advisors should come away with a clear understanding of:

- The level you are currently at and the achievements that help you to
  stand out
- Where you want to be in 12–18 months' time
- What you want to spend money on
- How that will help you to achieve your goals

If you're applying for larger sums of money, funders and external advisors expect you to go into more detail and your plans will be under more scrutiny. But never lose sight of the basic principle of outlining the journey funding will take you on and the impact it will have.

4 Budget tips

Be realistic: We know you're less likely to carry out plans without funding support. And we welcome ambitious activity that helps you to step up. But the costs you outline should be realistic and suited to the career position you are in now or want to be in in the next few months. For example, if your last video had 300 views, it's unlikely a funder will feel comfortable with you spending £5,000 on a music video. Or if your average gig fee is £100 it's probably not sustainable to spend £1,000 on each live show.

Using the 'details' box: Use any 'details' boxes to break down large headline costs. For example, instead of just saying Marketing and Promotion will cost £10,000, you should use any 'details' box to break this down (e.g. "PR (£x,xxx); Plugging (£y,yyy); Digital Marketing (£z,zzz)").

A balanced budget: Most funders need to see a balanced budget. A step-by-step way of getting this right is:

- Outline relevant activity costs in detail

- Add projected revenues from that activity (e.g. if you're spending money on recording and releasing an EP, add projected digital and/or physical revenue from that release)

- Add any income from other sources that you're willing to or able to invest (e.g. investment from a label, or support from other funders)

- The difference between the costs you outlined and the projected income is the amount you need to request from the funder. This amount allows your project to break even because of the funding support. For example, your total submitted expenditure may be £20,000. If before adding a request amount you are projecting income of £10,000, you would request £10,000 in grant support so that income equals expenditure and your budget balances

5 Involving and representing your clients

We all know that managers play a crucial role in the sector. When the relationship between a manager and an artist, writer or producer works, it's a beautiful thing and the role of grant funding in this relationship is mutually beneficial.

However, relationships can break down and the pandemic shone a light on some bad practices which – although rare – should be avoided. You must fully involve your client in funding applications. In some cases, only they can apply. In others their input is crucial and funders are looking to meet their needs primarily. You're doing your client a disservice and are highly unlikely to secure funding if they're not front and centre. And ultimately if you're applying on behalf of a client, you must not forget it's their money and any changes to plans need to be agreed by all parties

It is vital that managers applying for funding have a sense of perspective and understand that there are hundreds of other applicants who also meet eligibility criteria and also believe they are perfectly positioned for funding. Your reaction to a negative decision has a huge impact on your and might impact future funding applications. Take a measured approach and approach the feedback process in a constructive way.

Likewise, when you do secure grant support, let the funder know how the project is going and if the support is making a difference. It allows them to evolve their funds and champion successes, you can start to build a positive relationship for future deadlines or new clients.

MERCHANDISE (MERCH)

Over the years, there have been a number of artists for whom the merch table represents the largest part of their overall business. For many such hard-gigging bands and performers, the money made from T-shirt or poster sales can easily outstrip the revenues generated from the intellectual property of their songs or their recordings.

Typically, merchandise sales also sit outside of the terms of any contractual agreement with a promoter – although certain venues may attempt to charge artists a percentage of their merch sales (up to 25% plus VAT) for offering a concession to sell within their building. These practices are more common in larger corporate venues, although they have been challenged in recent years by organisations such as the Featured Artists Coalition – while some artists have attempted to circumvent their application by selling merchandise outside the venue or online.

As well as the potential revenue from selling clothing, posters, vinyl and other physical goods, merchandise is also an incredibly effective way for your artist to expand their brand and personality.

Logistically, and unless the venue provides someone, someone in the artist's team will need to work on the merch table and take responsibility for sales, stocktaking and looking after money. For small tours, that might be the tour manager; although for larger events, it's more likely someone will be employed specifically for this task.

Before that, you will also need someone to manufacture and supply your goods.

At the start of your artist's career, that is likely to be the artist themselves taking a DIY approach – however, as they gain an audience base and work with other partners, merchandising services can be provided by record labels or by third-party specialists capable of manufacturing on a "supply only" basis and therefore minimise wastage and over-stocking.

Once artists gain a certain level of popularity, specialist merchandise firms will also offer licensing partnerships – effectively licensing the artist's trademark or logo – and assume many of the risks involved in manufacturing, storing and selling products, whether that's on tour or online via the artist's website. As well as supplying retailers, these companies should also have specialist knowledge of selling merchandise outside of the UK, including shipping costs and any tax implications.

Under these partnerships, the merchandise company will typically pay an agreed royalty per item sold on tour. This is likely to be calculated on gross sales of a product's retail price (minus tax such as VAT, as well as any other pre-agreed deductions). It generally leaves a royalty rate of around 30% per item.

Alternatively, your artist could enter into a split-profit deal whereby merch sales are accounted for at a tour's conclusion and profits are split in the artist's favour – typically in a range of 75/25 or 80/20.

Of course, your artist can still go the DIY route, and assume the responsibility for merchandising. This will undoubtedly result in higher royalties, although with the added risk of manufacturing and storage, not to mention the challenge of updating designs and design concepts.

Increasingly, there are also strong environmental and ethical concerns about the production of merchandise, and a demand to ensure products are being manufactured under safe working practices and by methods that do not pollute the planet. Any reputable merchandiser should be able to answer your questions on these issues and provide evidence that goods are being produced in accordance with best ethical practices. See the section below on Climate Action for more information and sources of support.

LIVE SHOWS AS PROMOTION

Although not finance per se, live touring will typically open up opportunities for media and promotion – and thereby the means to stimulate other parts of an artist's business.

In the first instance, live touring is usually hooked around recorded activity (eg an album release) and will often be announced alongside – whether that's direct to media via a press release, or to an artist's existing fanbase via social media or email.

In itself, there's every chance that such announcements will generate radio plays and streaming activity; however the process of an artist travelling in-person to different national and international markets will also open doors to promotional opportunities (for instance, local radio appearances and sessions, or interviews with local media) as well as the possibility of in-store appearances at record shops – if your artist has the down time, energy and inclination.

With record shops increasingly diversifying into performance spaces in their own right, many artists will embark on what is effectively a "shadow tour" – scheduling daytime appearances in the towns and cities they are due to be playing later that evening. As well as an opportunity to push ticket sales, this kind of promotion can provide an effective and intimate way of exciting an artist's fanbase, as well as triggering sales of merchandise and chart eligible physical goods.

Some record shops will bundle in the price of a physical album with a ticket to meet the artist on their premises or to watch them return. This kind of activity might also encourage a label or distribution partner to help underwrite your artist's schedule and offer tour support.

Support Slots
Similar to your client guesting on another artist's track or being remixed by a well-known producer, playing support slots can provide an excellent way for your client to expand their audience base. Effectively, they are performing on somebody else's ticket.

Most upcoming artists will inevitably agree to play support to headline acts – either joining them for a string of dates on a tour, or for one-off appearances. Occasionally, headline acts will also look for local artists to open their shows.

It can be written into artist-promoter contracts that the artist has final say over the choice of support acts, as well as determining who pays for them – ie whether that's the promoter, or whether it comes out of the artist's guarantee as a show cost.

These slots can provide vital experience for your artist, allowing them to perform on larger stages to bigger crowds and in different geographical locations, as well as the added potential of building in promotional opportunities or the possibility to sell merchandise. But support slots can also be strategically important to more established artists – aligning them with younger artists and audiences in similar genres.

Many support opportunities will be determined by relationships – for example, a booking agent or label representing the same acts – and typically your artist will be paid a flat fee, alongside a limited rider, usually including an allocation of guest tickets. Again, this can be used strategically, in order to invite media or potential industry partners to watch your artist perform.

In other words, they can be an invaluable stepping stone.

Aside from fierce competition for the most desirable slots – and the probability that any payment will be limited – for these reasons an entrepreneurial manager can still derive many potential benefits for their artist from a well-considered and well-researched support appearance.

FESTIVALS

Aside from support slots, music festivals provide the other obvious opportunity for your artist to perform before new audiences. In the UK alone, there are now hundreds of outdoor events of every possible genre – from one-day events in major towns and cities, through to 4-day camping festivals in the countryside. The UK festival season stretches from May through to September and will incorporate a significant part of many artists' schedule.

Although some events will offer stages for upcoming acts and provide an application process for artists to pitch for slots, places on the more prominent stages are almost always determined via negotiations between agents and bookers – so yet another reason why your artist should employ a proactive agent with the connections and drive to push their live career forward.

Ideally, they will provide the leverage and know-how to help you navigate the festival market, locating most relevant opportunities to keep your artist's career in forward momentum – although, instinctively, both you and your artist should have a good idea of the kind of events where you'd want to perform.

Contractually, there can be differences with agreements between the festival and performers – all of which need to be agreed in advance between the manager and agent on behalf of the artist, and the promoter.

Ruth Barlow, Beggars Group's Director of Live Licensing

"In the last decade festivals increasingly see themselves as content providers or broadcasters. Often when performance offers come through, there's a myriad of requests involving recording, streaming, and archiving performances tethered to the artists' performance agreements. It's something we as a group of labels manage carefully. We weigh up and discuss opportunities on a case-by-case basis with artist managers and labels; if agreed, we contractually set boundaries about what can be recorded, where the recordings can be distributed and for how long.

In the past, festival broadcast requests tended to be tied to terrestrial national broadcasters in the territory. However with national broadcasters budgets slashed and costs increasing to deliver good quality recordings, these requests now often are tied into commercial partnerships and as a result most events want to broadcast online globally. Couple that notion with the number of festivals an artist can perform across a year and you have to question the value of a constant flow of live material being made available on services like YouTube and competing with an artist's 'official' recordings.

Since the pandemic the landscape has shifted slightly and we now strategically cherry pick the most impactful events in different territories and work together with the festivals to incorporate the live content they generate into our artists campaigns, which is working out to be beneficial for all parties."

For example:

- With multi-artist events, payment will typically be a one-off guaranteed fee.
- The event organiser will need to provide a more detailed itinerary – including production specs, stage times, load-in times, car parking and backstage facilities.
- Any accommodation (and associated costs) will have to be agreed in advance, including contact details for hotels and details of transportation to the event.

Because of the increased risks when playing outdoors, particularly in the UK, Force Majeure clauses are even more important. And especially in the context of COVID-19.

Other important considerations for a manager to consider are whether the organisers plan to record or broadcast the event. While this is becoming standard practice – i.e. for festivals to stream entire performances, or post clips on social media – it will have rights implications for your artist and any of their recording partners.

To receive songwriting royalties promptly, it is also essential that you supply PRS (or the collecting society your artist is registered with) and send them a full set list.

For more on this topic. MMF published an article with basic tips on playing at festivals which you can find on our website.

CREATING A TOURING BUDGET

As explained in Part One, agreeing a plan and then creating and managing a budget will be among a manager's key responsibilities when their artist is starting to build a live career.

Even at a basic level, overseeing a basic P&L (profit and loss) spreadsheet that balances revenues against costs and expenses will be hugely important – and this budget will ultimately determine all of your artist's touring plans, from the size of rooms they play to the cost of their production.

However, as touring gets more complicated and costly, the majority of managers will typically start working with the artist's accountant to develop touring plans and grow their live business.

Many accountants will, for instance, advise an artist to set up a separate limited company specifically for the live side of their business in order to mitigate some of the inherent risks when performing shows.

They will also be able to help structure the artist's live business and advise on what to budget for, how to create efficiencies in that budget and how to maximise potential revenue streams.

MMF members can access and download a number of helpful budget templates, but potential costs for an artist might include rehearsals and equipment hire, wages for the band and crew, travel and accommodation (including van hire), "per diems" (ie food/drink expenses for the touring party), insurance, agents fees and PRS payments.

Example touring budget

Sample tour costs

Artist
Touring where and when

BUDGET SUMMARY

		£	500.00
1	Travel	£	500.00
2	Hotels	£	500.00
3	Communication	£	500.00
4	Crew wages	£	500.00
5	Musicians' fees	£	500.00
6	Per diem	£	500.00
7	Transport	£	500.00
8	Sound & light	£	500.00
9	Production supplies	£	500.00
10	Rehearsals	£	500.00
11	Accountant	£	500.00
12	Legal/commissions	£	500.00
13	Insurance	£	500.00
14	Stationery	£	500.00
15	Sundries		

TOTAL	**£ 7,500.00**

Fees/income	£	1,000.00
Minus withholding tax @ ?%	£	200.00
Minus agent's commission 10%	£	100.00

Shortfall/profit   **-£ 6,800.00**

As already noted, these fixed costs of touring can be considerable – albeit they will ultimately be determined by the kind of artist you represent and the genre they operate in.

For instance, a DJ or solo performer might be able to scale back significantly on costs, while for a multi-piece band they might spiral substantially. Similarly, an artist who wishes to enjoy five-star luxury will ultimately have to pay for any largesse.

A good manager should be able to explain these facets of touring to their artist, and also set out the most important costs – in writing – including details of where financial responsibility starts and ends, whether that's the size of their guest list or the show production. Given the multiple people involved in putting on a live show, this is definitely a part of the business where it's helpful to have a paper trail.

A budget should, ideally, also have some sort of contingency strategy. As much as it's about setting up a plan and a routine, touring also involves the unexpected. Things break. Travel plans get derailed. People get sick. Revenues can be uncertain. So this is another area where the advice of an accountant will be invaluable.

As well as creating a budget, another key responsibility is to ensure that the tour operates to that budget – and that someone (in all likelihood the tour manager) is reporting back and reconciling costs and revenues on a daily basis, as well as keeping and saving receipts.

This latter point is especially important! Someone in the touring party has to take a daily responsibility for tracking and recording finances, and collecting receipts as you go along – whether those are being screenshotted by the tour manager on their mobile phone, or saved and deposited into envelopes. There are also a number of simple accountancy packages, where payments can be recorded, uploaded and stored online. Again, an accountant can advise on best practice here.

Keeping on top of these operational aspects of touring will not only enhance your ability to make educated decisions and react to any problems or additional costs that occur on the road, it will also make your life much easier when it comes to settling accounts. When accounts have to be filed, no one wants to scrabble around looking for proof of a petrol receipt or hotel bill.

The majority of artists will be focussed and consumed by the creative side of performing. They'll want their manager, and their extended team, to ensure the mechanics underpinning those performances are functioning properly and to budget.

From a manager's perspective, that also means turning over every stone in order to make savings and efficiencies, whether that's finding the best deals for accommodation and food or ensuring that shows are routed in the most cost effective way possible.

TOURING INSURANCE

Another key consideration for a manager is to ensure the artist is fully insured.

You can guarantee that promoters and venues will have insurance in place (or they should have) but given the fact (i) a number of people on tour are effectively working for your artist; and (b) touring is risky and unpredictable, it would be hugely negligent to embark on live shows without adequate cover in place.

From a legal and regulatory perspective your artist will need to have employers liability insurance. This should cover all of your core team (including freelancers) that are working on a tour.

However, in addition to this, the majority of venues – and certainly larger venues – will insist that you also take out public liability insurance.

There are a number of highly experienced brokers who specialise in music insurance, most of whom are Associate members of the MMF.

All will be able to offer tailored advice about the kind of insurance you'd require, and what this would cover – for instance, as well as protecting the individuals your artist employs, it can also stretch to protect instruments, computers, amplifiers, merchandise and personal effects.

Importantly, you can also extend insurance to cover your artist while they're recording or rehearsing, mitigating the risk of equipment being stolen or damaged.

The cost of insurance will be dependent upon the scale of your touring, but it is vital that you arrange payments and premiums in advance and also develop a good working relationship with your broker.

Emergencies rarely happen at the most convenient moments, and if you do need to activate your insurance policy it might be in a last minute situation.

Insurance with Molly Puttman from Music Insurance Brokers

Insurance is often the last thing on people's lists but becomes the most important when something goes wrong. Below are some key points to consider, especially if your artists are going out on tour:

- Is their kit covered? Do they own any equipment, or even a laptop that they work on? It's probably cheaper than you think to insure this and will definitely be worth it if anything were to get broken or be stolen and have to be replaced. You can replace the kit straight away and claim the money back meaning there's no break in being able to tour, record etc.

- Are they hiring kit or being loaned kit by a sponsor? It is part of standard hire or sponsor agreements that they are responsible for any equipment/kit while it is in their possession and they'll be responsible for the replacement cost if anything is damaged or stolen. It's really important that you get cover in place in advance of receiving the kit so that they aren't left with a costly bill if there's an accident or theft.

- Do they have Public Liability cover? It's a requirement of many venues and festivals that artists have at least a basic level (usually £2 or £5 million) of Public Liability cover. It covers them in case their actions lead to the damage of third party property or bodily injury of a third party. This can be something as simple as spilling a drink over a mixing desk or as serious as causing a physical injury to a festival-goer. Accidents happen and this cover gives you peace of mind in case they end up responsible for one.

- Do they employ anyone? If you are a direct employee of your artist or they employ anyone that works under their instruction or guidance then it is best to have Employers Liability cover. This comes at a standard limit of £10 million and provides cover for claims brought against your artist by their employees following an injury at work. It becomes a legal requirement if they have a limited company with two or more directors so please do get in touch if you'd like to discuss your artist's specific situation.

- Are they starting to get paid or paying out a lot to tour? Either way you may want to consider getting this covered. We can cover costs/expenses or guarantees for cancellation/non-appearance. This means that if your artist is ill, injured, dies or cannot get to a show due to unavoidable travel delay you can either claim the costs or the guarantees to put you back in a situation as if the show had gone ahead (depending on which option is insured). There are also options to cover adverse weather for outdoor shows, terrorism, civil commotion and other extensions. It is worth noting that to cover outdoor shows we need at least two weeks' notice and it's best to get shows on cover as far in advance as possible to ensure you're covered if anything were to go wrong.

- Are they travelling? Sounds obvious but travel insurance is often overlooked, if they were to suffer a medical emergency when abroad this is the policy that would cover the expense. It also covers trip cancellation, baggage delay, personal items and more. It's often best to have an annual policy that covers them for all trips Worldwide.

EUROPEAN TOURING AND BREXIT

Before Brexit, touring in mainland Europe was a relatively straightforward enterprise with little in the way of bureaucracy and red tape. Beyond the basic logistical challenges of working abroad – such as driving on the "wrong side of the road – artists would simply have to load up splitter van, or jump on a plane, or the Eurostar, get to the show and meet the terms of a promoter's contract.

Plotting and budgeting for a European tour was relatively straightforward, while European festivals represented a major opportunity to perform before new audiences. Aside from a handful of non-EU territories, such as Switzerland, terms like "carnet" or "visa" were applicable to a bygone era.

This has all now changed, and is subject to further change, as and when agreements are reached between the UK Government and EU countries on issues such as free movement of labour and exemptions for cultural workers.

The latest Government guidance can be found on the Gov.UK website and the members section of the MMF has a number of updated resources aimed directly at managers. The Musicians Union has also produced a useful flowchart guide.

However, at the time of writing, any UK manager with an artist intending to perform in our most important international trading bloc (ie an EU country, or Switzerland, Norway, Iceland or Liechtenstein) will need to prepare and check thoroughly for the latest details around the following:

- A valid passport, at least 6 months before expiry.
- A carnet for your equipment obtained from your Chamber of Commerce.
- Potentially an EORI number for any merch you are planning to sell, plus a goods reference number if you are transporting it by van both available on Gov.uk.
- A valid UK driving licence, if you are intending to drive.
- Healthcare and travel insurance cover.
- Equipment insurance.

Visas

Although many EU countries do not require visas for short-term touring, some will do – including Croatia, Portugal, Cyprus, Malta and Bulgaria. The ISM has created a valuable country-by-country breakdown, listing the current requirements for permits free on its website.

Duration of stay

Although UK citizens have a waiver to stay for 90 days within any 180 days, individual countries may have different rules in regards to working within their borders which may impact artists on residencies. For example, in the Netherlands you can work for no more than 6 weeks in every 13 weeks without applying for work permits, in Switzerland only 8 days per year, and in Norway only 14 days per year. In Sweden, artists are permitted to travel visa-free only with an invitation from an established event organiser.

Carnets

A carnet is effectively a "passport for goods". When crossing an EU border with instruments, music and DJ equipment or lighting, you will need an ATA Carnet from the London Chamber of Commerce and Industry in order to pass smoothly through customs. These are valid for a year and can also be used internationally outside of the EU.

An ATA Carnet for £10,000 worth of instruments will typically cost several hundred pounds, although the MU & FAC recently announced a special discounted rate. There is also a helpful guide on where to get your carnet stamped at Dover / Calais on the MMF website resources section.

Cabotage

Cabotage is the transport of goods or passengers between two places in the same country by a transport operator from another country for the purposes of hire and reward. A third country registered vehicle under these rules may only make 3 stops in mainland Europe – a major issue for touring which normally goes beyond 3 dates in the EU.

Large concert haulage companies have lobbied for a solution and been granted the right to dual registration of vehicles (in the EU and UK) to get round this rule which has come at an increased cost. Fortunately it has now been confirmed that self-drive splitter vans (transporting both goods and people) are not covered by the cabotage rules and can therefore do more than 3 stops without breaching the law.

Since August 2022 for freight (where a driver is driving goods they don't own) you will also need a Goods Movement Reference Number to cross the border, you can generate this yourself via the Gov.uk website using your carnet number and details of your crossing.

Taxes

If your artists are self-employed UK tax payers and travelling to Europe to work temporarily, they are advised to fill in the A1 government form in order to reduce or avoid any doubling up of social security payments. Some managers have found issues with payment sole traders in France by promoters and have been advised that using a limited company for touring avoids this. Please check with any promoter you are working with before the tour on the current situation.

Merchandise

If you are taking merchandise from the UK to sell in Europe, you will be expected to declare these goods and pay import duty (if applicable) and VAT in advance of crossing the border depending on the rules of origin and total value of the goods.

If you are taking commercial goods in your baggage to the EU, Switzerland, Norway, Iceland or Liechtenstein, to sell or bringing them back to the UK to sell you must check the customs requirements in the country you're travelling to. You'll also need to declare your goods to customs.

As a result of these complications, some managers are exploring the potential of using European merchandise companies to provide goods and fulfil services but this clearly comes at a cost and eats into margins.

D2C Stores

The MMF understands that the most popular D2C stores (such as Ochre, Bandcamp, Music Glue etc) have changed their T&Cs to pass the cost of import duty onto the consumer from the seller (the artist). However, this is an area with a real lack of clarity, and we advise that managers speak to us for the latest developments.

So How to Make EU Touring Viable?

All this bureaucracy comes at a cost and requires additional planning and often additional days planned into a touring schedule to prepare for potential border delays. Yet managers and artists are innovative people and find ways to make touring work. Many are reporting that artists are travelling with carry-on instruments only which don't need a carnet and then hiring backline locally within the EU. Some are also hiring musicians/dancers/performers locally although this requires additional rehearsals.

MUSIC & CLIMATE ACTION

While the onus of climate change does not fall on an individual artist, and action must be a collective response, there are various steps an artist team can take to minimise climate impact and practice sustainability. The Music Climate Pact states that "By aligning as a sector, we stand to de-politicise sustainability and address our biggest environmental impacts in an efficient and collaborative way."

Managers are encouraged to sit down with their artists and talk about ways to reduce carbon emissions across their activities, and then build relationships with partners who have aligned values and commitment towards sustainability.

In a report published in 2022, Music Declare Emergency estimated that 82% of music fans expressed concern about climate change and global warming.

Sustainable Live Touring
Travel is typically the largest offender when it comes to carbon emissions from live events.

Ecolibrium has an in-depth guide on sustainable travel for artists and the music industry which includes points such as reducing touring party numbers, taking more direct flights, and travelling by coach or train for EU tours.

Although this is not a major point of concern for artists who tour locally, it is important to keep in mind. As your artists begin to expand their touring territories, it will invariably increase their carbon emission.

Artists can measure their carbon footprint using free carbon accounting tools such as Ecolibrium's Travel Carbon Calculator which enables artists to log their travel details, record miles and associated carbon footprints, and take appropriate steps to offset carbon.

Julie's Bicycle provides a template for a 'green rider' which has a list of suggestions such as making information available via the ticket agent to the audience about travel options such as carpool, public transport and cycling thus minimising fuel consumption.

Artists can also request for certain items to be removed from their rider. The BYOBottle campaign for instance calls to minimise plastic pollution by encouraging artists to bring reusable bottles to shows.

Artists can include some or all of the points depending on the size and venue of the show.

"The music industry broadly needs to take this seriously and we as managers have a responsibility to make choices about our artists' supply chains that are as environmentally friendly as possible!"

Hannah Partington, Young Artists

Merch and Physical

Discuss environmental policy with your supplier or manufacturer, and where possible choose partners that use renewable energy at their premises and adopt a commitment to sustainability. This approach can be applied to both merchandise companies as well as physical record manufacturers.

Merchandise is an integral part of an artist campaign, and not selling merch at all is not a practical option. However, thoughtful merch production and distribution can minimise climate damage. Consider the kind of merch you are selling. Can you swap plastic key rings for a signed copy of a print made out of recycled materials? When producing t-shirts, opt for companies that use recycled or organic cotton.The Ethical Tee is one such company providing eco-friendly alternatives.

Manufacturers such as Key Production champion sustainability and offer vinyl production with sustainable materials at competitive pricing, This neither affects sound quality, nor consumer experience. Similarly, CD jewel cases have a high manufacturing footprint, whereas card sleeves have a 95% lower carbon footprint and are much cheaper to make!

Some other points to keep in mind – try to manufacture locally where you can, don't overstock, minimise packaging such as shrink wrap in the mail order, and reduce stops in the merchandise journey e.g. ship directly to distributors from pressing plants rather than via a distribution centre.

Education and Communication

The climate issue largely revolves around education and awareness, and the music industry is uniquely positioned such that it can inspire immense change through direct fan communication. A simple and effective step an artist can take is to educate themselves on the issues and integrate the sustainability message into their fan communications.

The Music Industry Climate Pack from MDE is a great comprehensive beginner's resource for all those in the music industry. Artists can also take part in specific media training to enable themselves to speak with confidence and precision on such topics whilst avoiding pitfalls.

Encourage labels to build in the cost of offsetting the carbon footprint into the budget, as well as introduce a line into future contracts agreeing to work together on the climate and ecological emergency.

When your artist is at a stage in their career at which frequent travel becomes essential, balance your unavoidable emissions with donations towards climate positive charities and initiatives.

All in all, ensure you are proactive with your approach to sustainability. As we head towards a dawning climate emergency, engaging with sustainable practice will become less of a choice. You don't need to be an expert – just take basic, small steps. Talk to other managers, share ideas, and ask for help.

MENTAL HEALTH ON THE ROAD

Although live music is one of the most exciting and compelling parts of management, there's no doubt that touring and travelling, combined with long days, long nights and a discombobulating schedule, can test relationships to their limit.

There can be a huge disconnect from the adrenaline rush and excitement of being onstage, to the more mundane aspects of touring.

Aside from the pressures on your artist to perform, and to be in the right headspace to perform, the rest of your team will also have to deal with stresses – from the tour manager and production manager on the road, to those behind the scenes. For every sell-out show that goes right and where the audience is receptive, there will inevitably be others that go wrong – where things get broken or lost, people get sick, or tickets that don't sell.

As a manager, it is unlikely you will be on the road for the duration of a tour.

However, in collaboration with your team, you will still want to make provisions for everyone's mental health – and ensure that planning and scheduling makes time for rest, food and personal space.

For further reference, please see the MMF's Guide To Mental Health, which contains signposting to support organisations and help lines and hugely helpful resources on the Tour Production Group website.

PART 3

Scaling Up & Going Global

If getting a music management business off the ground can sometimes appear like a plate-spinning exercise, operating globally and plugging your client into international markets represents a whole new level. As well as navigating different cultures, languages and business practices, it also means exciting potential to build new networks and new partnerships.

For many managers, the experience can almost feel like starting again.

Undoubtedly it will also put additional pressures on your client. The cycle of creation, performance and promotion can be relentless, while release campaigns can appear never-ending, with artists also expected to feed the constant demands of social media and marketing. Add to this the pressure of working between time zones and an expectancy to remain "on brand", it's little wonder that there's such a heightened awareness around mental health and ways to support artists with these pressures, whether that's structuring "time out" in their schedule, or ensuring they are provided with resources for health and well-being, whether that's a personal trainer, a nutritionist, a stylist, a driver or security.

Building an extended team will likely be more of a necessity than a practicality. It might also mean reconstructing your own business or working in partnership with another manager.

Depending on your client, much of this groundwork might already be underway. For instance, they may already be signed to a major record label or publisher with offices in key territories, or working with an US booking agent. But even at a basic level, any artist making their music and repertoire available on a streaming service is effectively operating in an international market.

In itself, the ability to collect and analyse the growing range of consumer data generated from streaming and social media has provided an enormous asset for music managers – and one that can greatly enhance decision making.

Seeing a spike of interest in Germany or North America? Then you can focus resources on a PR in Berlin or Los Angeles, or booking some shows in Munich or New York. Similarly, a playlist placement, album review, radio play or collaboration might trigger interest somewhere else in the world. Indeed, there are numerous examples of UK artists (Rag N Bone Man and Lewis Capaldi being the most obvious) who broke in international markets before gaining traction at home. Elsewhere, entire genres, for instance dance or electronic music, are almost entirely predicated on their international appeal.

These routes to success are so innumerable, and the possibilities so endless, that it felt counter-productive to replicate the details of Parts One and Two. So instead, we have aimed to explore a number of areas that the majority of music managers will have to consider when looking at stepping up and expanding their operations.

We hope that you find this of practical use, and also look forward to receiving feedback and input that we can use to expand future editions of this text.

CHAPTER 9

Growing Your Management Company

I n addition to expanding your live, recording and publishing partners, there will undoubtedly be a range of other opportunities for income generation that come as a result of managing an act with international appeal. It is also likely you will look to expand your own management business. This might involve bringing in new staff and offering new services, but also potentially restructuring your operations or collaborating with other managers, partners and investors.

At the very least, it is likely that you will employ a personal assistant or day-to-day manager who can provide support for administrative tasks such as diary management, scheduling, and planning, as well as deal with incoming enquiries.

However, some of the more advanced models – all of which are referenced in the MMF publication series Managing Expectations – include:

Operating Under the Umbrella of Another Management Company
Some larger management companies operate an umbrella-style structure, offering a range of in-house services and expertise (e.g. digital marketing, legal, accounting, touring, brand partnerships, investment diary or "day to day" management assistance or simply office space and allyship) while actively encouraging independent managers to work with them.

This can be a mutually beneficial arrangement for both parties – enabling mature management businesses to bring in fresh talent and expand the range of artists they collaborate with, while allowing independent managers to retain autonomy and grow their activities. Importantly, this arrangement can also help independent managers to expand their networks and ensure they remain connected to other like minded individuals.

How these arrangements are structured will vary from company to company. Some managers will continue to operate independently but contribute financially to a central collective pot; while others might prefer the benefits of a regular baseline salary, while contributing an agreed percentage of any commission earned to the company they are working under.

Co-Management
Another tried and tested method of expanding your business is to join forces with another manager, and either forging a new partnership and setting up a new company, merging your companies or collaborating together as separate businesses for a specific client.

These kinds of partnerships can work particularly well if each manager has different skill sets – for instance, if one comes from a background in recorded music and the other has experience in live music – or if you are based in different geographical locations. It is not uncommon for a UK manager to work in tandem with a US manager, and to pool their expertise and networks. Similarly, there are a number of UK-based managers who partner with US-based managers and represent their artists solely for the UK and Europe.

This kind of co-management approach can pay commercial dividends, and either help share your workload and ensure it remains manageable, or, if you are taking on an international client, expand your existing business. Taking such a proactive approach, and ensuring your artist has agreed additional global representation, can also reduce the risk of your client being surreptitiously courted by overseas managers.

As with any partnership, it is imperative that you seek advice from your lawyer and accountant, setting out a clear delineation of responsibilities, financial agreements and obligations should you choose to stop working together in the future. Considering the implications of how the partnership might dissolve, what conflict resolutions could be agreed in advance and how sunset clauses will be upheld.

Hiring Expertise
As your business expands, it is also likely you will bring in extra staff – both to assist you in operations and to specialise in specific growth areas. Some managers

will hire staff to work specifically for a certain client as their designated "day-to-day", making that individual a first point of contact and delegating operations and duties and building them into the company. Others might prefer to contribute by outsourcing a specific skill (for instance, digital marketing, brand partnerships, promotional appearances or touring) that help grow or expand the manager's core overall business, or keep certain responsibilities in-house. Others might reflect on their own skill set and look more for assistance in areas of business administration so they can remain at the coal face of the artists business and practice of management

As with overseeing a team of partners, hiring and retaining staff for your business – while keeping them motivated and happy – is a skill in itself, and demands a long-term commitment to welfare, development and training.

Some of the most progressive management companies, such as YMU Music, who were recognised for Team Achievement at the 2021 Artist & Manager Awards and also Young Artists, have gone out of their way to promote inclusivity initiatives – providing staff with professional developments and well-being facilities, and offering provision to support resilience and positive mental health.

Developing Additional Specialist Services
Another increasingly common route for expansion is for a management company to develop a specialism beyond its core services, and then to offer this as an additional service for their own management clients – or as a standalone service for external clients.

For example, a management company might onboard a consultant with expertise in developing partnerships with brands, and with the expertise to deliver fully-licensed campaigns. These activities might be beyond the scope of the contractual agreement with their existing clients, and so they might charge an additional consultancy fee for any brand-related work they undertake.

Similarly, it might provide the management company an opportunity to expand their business, and offer these services to other management companies.

FUNDING & RAISING CAPITAL

In order to grow, all businesses rely on funding, investment and finance – and your management company will be no different. While revenues from your services will provide the bulk of your income, success can also open opportunities to raise finance that might help expand and further your commercial goals.

Traditionally, the most popular route to raising finance has been through a bank loan. Although theoretically a straightforward process, many creative businesses encounter resistance when attempting to access finance – and particularly those whose value is based on personal relationships or networks, rather than tangible ownership of property or intellectual property.

There is also the possibility of seeking outside investment for your management business in return for an ownership stake. This is actually relatively common, especially if that investor can bring with them an additional expertise or specialism or are able to open new doors and opportunities to help you grow.

In order to encourage inward investment, successive Governments have supported a number of 'tax-efficient' initiatives that offer incentives for investors to put more money into the high growth creative and digital sectors.

Probably the best known of these are the Seed Enterprise Investment Scheme (SEIS) and Enterprise Investment Scheme (EIS).

The SEIS is aimed predominantly at start-ups and allows them to receive investment of up to £150,000. Among the qualifying criteria are stipulations that the company has gross assets under £200,000, and less than 25 employees. Investors can benefit by claiming income tax relief of 50% on any sum up to £100,000 invested in a tax year.

The EIS is similar, but aimed at more established companies – allowing them to raise up to £5m each year, to a maximum of £12m in total. Qualifying companies must not have gross assets worth more than £15m and fewer than 250 full-time equivalent employees. Investors are incentivised by claiming income tax relief of 30% on any sum of up to £1m invested in a tax year.

Your accountant will advise on how you can benefit from these schemes, or any other relevant investment opportunities.

For those in the fortunate position of managing a highly successful artist, you may also be called upon to help advise on your client's wealth management, potentially expanding on opportunities for collaboration, growth and entrepreneurialism.

BRAND PARTNERSHIPS – THE NEXT LEVEL

As mentioned in the previous chapter, alongside an accountant's expertise for financial planning and investments, there are also the extracurricular opportunities brought by fame – and particularly from brands looking for endorsements or collaborations. For certain artists, brand partnerships represent the most financially important aspect of their business, and can frequently underpin their other creative work – for example, by helping finance touring or recording plans, or enabling the artist to explore other creative ground outside of music.

It is here that a manager's guiding hand will be crucial, both filtering incoming requests and forging relationships with potential partners, and ensuring the artist's integrity is protected.

For many brands, music offers exposure through authenticity and credibility. It offers access to culture and ready-made audiences, and especially so if they can collaborate directly in the creation of an asset or experience. In the social media age, brands also increasingly want a direct relationship with the talent they work alongside.

This represents a major shift in terms of how artist-brand relationships are structured – and rather than being brokered by a label or other intermediary, as they were historically, there is enormous potential for the brand to operate as another creative partner in their own right. This becomes even more impactful if the artist has a genuine affinity for the product they are endorsing, and can even result in them setting up in business together. Examples include Rihanna and LVMH (Fenty & Fenty Beauty), Dr. Dre and Apple (Beats by Dre), Diddy and Diageo (Ciroc Vodka), Pharrell and Chanel (The Chanel-Pharrell Collection) or Kanye West and Adidas (Yeezy).

As a consequence, rather than face historic accusations of "selling out", these days an intelligent and well-considered brand partnership is arguably more likely to empower an artist to be less compromising by opening lucrative income streams. In addition to the financial incentives, in many instances it can also further their art and creativity.   Gorillaz for example in 2017 with the drive of their management company, Eleven Management , negotiated several brand partnerships with Chelsea Football Club, Nike, E.On, Jaguar Land Rover, Red Bull, Deutsche Telecom, Sonos, Hennessey and YouTube to help Damon Albarn and Jamie Hewlett bring their creative visions to life.

For a manager, understanding the tangible worth of such intangible qualities as their client's "brand" and "identity" is hugely important. While possible to protect certain elements of these qualities through trade marks (which can encompass any combination of words, sounds, logos or colours) these effectively act as your currency for the exploitation of any ancillary rights, and may need to be substantiated or made credible by data – whether that's social media activity, ticket sales, streams or any other relevant metric.

Alongside brand partnerships, digital innovations also offer many possibilities for an artist to fund and expand their business – and particularly with the advent of

Web3 and emergence of new types of digital products such as NFTs ("non-fungible tokens").

This is a fascinating, volatile, fast-moving and disruptive sector. Although still in its infancy, it is likely to offer certain artists an opportunity to serve specific audience segments who crave and value digital products – in much the same way that other fans might treasure vinyl or physical merchandise. There is also clear potential for an artist to develop hybrid products, where physical items are authenticated or personalised by NFTs, or where digital ownership can open up specific rewards or access to the purchaser.

This could have a revolutionary impact in areas like ticketing, as well as financing and the all important ownership. Some artists and managers are already experimenting with crowdfunded models, whereby fans can purchase an ownership stake in a composition or track, and then share in the future revenues.

It is also a sector susceptible to great changes, with new entrepreneurs and products continually entering the space, and ongoing concerns around the reported environmental damage caused by some blockchain-related innovations, and where the involvement of some of the bigger DSPs is likely to have further game-changing impacts.

CHAPTER 10

Going Global

RECORDING & PUBLISHING DEALS

Working in a truly global recorded market, with differences and idiosyncrasies between individual territories and countries, is a truly exciting prospect and one where there can be major disparities between the popularity of different service types – for instance, between paid and ad-supported subscription platforms – or even tastes in how music is consumed.

In France, for example, homegrown streaming service Deezer remains a hugely significant player. In Germany and Japan, uptake to streaming has been relatively slow, but sales of physical formats have remained relatively robust. In South Korea, the most prominent music streaming platforms include Melon, Genie Music, YouTube Music, Flo and Naver Vibe.

In Ghana, a market of strategic importance for many UK artists, the majority of recorded revenue comes from mobile ringtone and ringback sales. In Nigeria, Boomplay is among the biggest services. In China, the recorded market is dominated by TenCent and NetEase, offering a hybrid of streaming, downloads, live streaming and karaoke.

Such developments have undoubtedly shifted mindsets between what might be considered a "developed" or "developing" music market.

The world's biggest superstars are now as likely to come from South Korea or Puerto Rico as they are from the UK or the US. Meanwhile, territories like Latin America have undoubtedly been elevated in importance. Mexico City, for instance, was declared by Spotify in 2018 as the world's "streaming Mecca", and by ChartMetric as the number one "Trigger City" due to its voracious appetite for streaming.

Capitalising on these changes undoubtedly presents a challenge to managers and their clients, and will be key consideration for many artists and songwriters if they decide to sign to a major label or publisher. These companies enjoy the scale of a global network, with offices and partners around the world. They can synchronise and schedule a global release campaign across multiple territories and in multiple languages, albeit they will aim to control a greater share of an artist's rights and revenues.

Similarly, the biggest independent labels will also offer ready-made networks of distribution, marketing and promotion, with "boots on the ground" in all significant markets.

However, for more entrepreneurial managers and artists, there is clearly potential to move outside of traditional structures and work with a distributor or label services company who will deliver your artist's music to retail, while bringing in specialist marketing, promotional and PR support on a territorial basis – and increasing that level of support as and when your artist starts to gain traction.

As with other aspects of management, there is a trade off here.

Signing away rights to a record label can bring benefits in terms of expertise, support and a reduced workload, as well plugging your artist into a ready-made international network; while retaining those rights might increase the manager's workload, but ensure the artist receives a greater share of revenue and greater long-term control over their career.

The latter option also provides the artist with greater flexibility, and potentially greater leverage, should they want to sign with a label later down the line.

Rather than sign away their rights in perpetuity to a record label, it is now more commonplace for artists, and especially the most popular artists with the most leverage, to licence their rights exclusively for a finite period. Such a strategy can result in the best of both worlds – allowing the artist to benefit from the international support structures of a record label, while retaining overall control of their recordings. It also leaves open the possibility of renegotiating deal terms or working with a new partner whenever that licensing deal runs out.

In this scenario, the label assumes the role of a "rights partner" rather than a "rights owner", Developing a global-facing strategy can include many other considerations.

As well as incorporating different languages, time zones and business practices, there are also creative opportunities. For instance, a manager might help their artist to engage in a mutually beneficial collaboration with an overseas artist – providing a guest verse, or remixing a track – or they might aim for a booking at a specific festival, or promotion in a certain magazine.

In many ways, taking your client global can be like starting again with the manager looking to fill in gaps or find additional resources and expertise. Ultimately, this might result in a management company expanding and opening offices in key international markets or bringing onboard consultants based in those territories.

These trends in recorded music are also relevant to the music publishing sector, which is now commonly being redefined under the more proactive brand of "song management" – with writers, producers and managers now able to assume far greater control over song catalogues, and being provided with the tools and services to strike their own sub-licensing agreements with international partners.

In the future, it feels that managers will only become more active in driving forward these kinds of business structures, helping their clients establish their own labels or publishing companies, while plugging into international services and expertise.

The Right to Audit

All deals should include the right for the artist to audit be that their label, publisher or any other entity with whom they sign a contract. This will ensure they are being paid correctly according to the contractual terms of their deal. Managers may be concerned about using audit rights as they worry it could damage relationships with their artists. However auditing is an important tool to build trust. If an audit finds zero or very few errors then this can rebuild relationships. On the other hand if an audit finds significant underpayments there is often a settlement to be paid and assurances this won't happen again. Some managers with significant artists audit regularly – every 5 years minimum.

"In 46 years in the music business I have yet to hear of any audit of a label or publisher that has not found money payable to the artist. I have never audited and found that my artist owed money conversely. Audit should be part of any manager's business plan."

Paul Crockford, Crockford Management

Finding an Auditor

There are some specialist music auditing firms. Your artist's accountant may have an audit team in house or be able to recommend one and the MMF can also help with connections. For some the cost of auditing can be too costly (around £5k+), however many managers say in their experience they have always found more money missing than the cost of the audit so it pays its way. Several managers have mentioned the benefit of ensuring that the label/publisher needs to provide receipts for costs charged to the artist's account during the audit process.

RENEGOTIATION & RECOUPMENT

A good deal of current artists will have signed their first album deals in a pre-digital (pre-2000's) or early digital era (2000s). These early deals, which were most likely in perpetuity, are unlikely to have specifically mentioned digital income or if they did it may be quite vague with references to downloads rather than streaming. Many managers and lawyers have argued that in the absence of specific provisions streaming income should be treated as a licence not a sale and therefore be subject to a 50% royalty. Others argue that as streaming is part broadcast, part on demand it should incur a form of equitable remuneration as does radio play.

Whichever perspective you agree with, countless artists will come to a point where their royalty rate feels outdated and should be revised and updated for a digital era. Whilst successful artists may have been able to renegotiate their contracts this century, many will not have had sufficient leverage and even may still be unrecouped (paying back their advance/other costs attributed to their account) meaning they see no income whatsoever for the streaming of their music decades later.

The MMF, along with the Featured Artists Coalition, have long advocated on these issues and thanks also to the FixStreaming and Broken Record campaigns, there has been a significant ramp up in pressure on the labels to address artists discontent. Resulting from this pressure all three major labels have followed the lead of Beggars to since disregard unrecouped balances pre-2000 (although only Sony has done this on a rolling 20 year basis).

However fair digital royalty rates remain unaddressed and in some cases can be at extremely low levels based on physical rates as low as >10%. In the US the 35 year reversion right seems to have stimulated more recent renegotiation of royalties, even if few artists have got their catalogues back entirely, but this is not the case in the UK.

Artists who enjoy an increase in popularity – and therefore an increase in leverage – will be tempted to either seek improved terms of existing deals, or even to push for a reversion of rights. For instance, an artist might agree to extend their current deal in exchange for an improved royalty rate on previous releases – or sometimes the enticement of a re-release campaign can be enough to open up a sensible discussion on rates in exchange for promotion – leading to a win-win for both parties. With catalogues reaching ever higher valuations, and with ongoing controversies around the application of historic contractual terms to new forms of music consumption, such amendments can have significant implications.

In any event the MMF and FAC will be encouraging labels to look at fair minimum rates for digital income, regardless of negotiating power of the artists, given the huge success of catalogue on streaming and the need for all to share in the return to growth of the recorded music sector in the digital age.

LEGACY & CATALOGUE MANAGEMENT

As mentioned above, the more unforeseen dynamics of streaming and social media has been the new life breathed into music catalogue. The infinite "shelf space" provided by DSPs has resulted in universal access to the entire history of music, while products released decades ago compete on its own terms with the latest tracks and albums.

This huge pool of music is also susceptible to a whole variety of external factors – for instance a well-placed sync, social media algorithms, a viral video campaign, or a news item – which can potentially trigger or ignite interest in a certain track or artist, and often with career-change impact, introducing them to a whole new audience.

These phenomena are now occurring on a daily basis, some as a result of a carefully contrived strategy, others by simply by happy accident. Some of the more high profile examples would be Rick Astley and "Rickrolling", the soundtracking of Kate Bush in Stranger Things, the TikTok mash-ups of Fleetwood Mac's Dreams, the Shangri-La's meme machine "Remember (Walking In The Sand)" or the global impact of Verzuz live streams during lockdown for artists including Brandy, Babyface or Gladys Knight.

Along with soundtracks and biopics, all have resulted in resonance and ripple effects – and a renewed reassessment in the value of music catalogues.

For managers, the knock-on impact has been considerable.

For those working for talent at the start of their careers, who are helping artists, songwriters and producers create a body of work, it has re-emphasised the importance of rights ownership and ensuring licensing partnerships with record labels and music publishers are future-proofed and structured to protect their long-term interests. A song or a track might only realise its true worth many years after it was released.

For managers representing clients who have already created a catalogue of work, it has opened new opportunities to exploit those rights and revalue their artist's legacy.

At the top end of the scale, we have also witnessed a whole series of catalogue acquisitions, led by companies such as Hipgnosis Songs, Round Hill Music and Primary Wave, alongside the major labels and publishers, where investors are defining music rights as an "asset class" and purchasing outright the publishing or recording rights (and sometimes the publishing *and* recording rights) of iconic superstar artists – including those who are no longer alive.

This trend has further inflated the value of catalogue, and the perceived value of music estates and legacies; to the point that we now talk about "song management" or "rights management" as a discipline in its own right, and the ability of a custodian to extract ever greater value from music rights, while nurturing and protecting their long-term brand value.

As well as more standard exploitations of rights – for instance, the biopics *Rocket Man* or *Bohemian Rhapsody*, which took the music of Elton John and Queen to new audiences, while repositioning their legacies, and dramatically increasing streams and ticket sales – there can be hugely lucrative avenues for managers to explore with merchandise, live shows, reissues, brands, sync deals and digital partnerships.

Even artists and songwriters who are no longer active can benefit from this kind of highly-focussed and highly targeted approach to repertoire management – as can the relatives and beneficiaries of artists who have passed away.

As detailed in Eamonn Forde's 2021 book, *Leaving The Building: The Lucrative Afterlife of Music Estates*, while the affairs for some of the world's biggest artists have, particularly in the past, been left in a state of disarray, far more importance is now placed on legacy management. Some artists feel incredibly strongly about this issue – for instance, not wanting certain material to be re-released or their music to be associated with certain brands. Aspects of an artist's career that may have appeared trivial or minor when they were alive – including audio visual material, emails and social media messages, photographs, demos, letters, clothes, instruments – can assume far greater value after their death.

For this reason, managers of artists with a substantial catalogue will be expected to have discussions with their clients to at least consider a legacy strategy –

determining the ownership of rights and, effectively, to establish who runs and benefits from their business after they have died.

In a digital environment, where all repertoire competes on the same platform and holograms can perform live, the impact of an artist can extend way beyond their lifetime.

INTERNATIONAL TOURING

The global dynamics of streaming have impacted significantly on the business of live music – introducing artists to international audiences at a far earlier stage in their development, and helping feed demand for those artists to perform at shows and festivals. The data generated by streaming has also opened up knowledge and access to touring markets, particularly across Asia, Africa and Central and South America, and given managers and agents greater confidence to plot touring activity around audience engagement.

For managers this can be a double-edged sword.

While having consumer demand for your artist is clearly a positive, the process of navigating overseas markets and incorporating international touring to your business strategy opens up a whole range of logistical and financial challenges. And particularly so in regards to North America – the world's biggest and most lucrative music market, but notoriously the most challenging and expensive to conquer.

Although many artists start to perform internationally relatively quickly, and especially in key cities such as New York, LA, Paris and Berlin, having team structure in place will be invaluable – especially as your artist is likely to be starting further down the ladder, and might be playing to unfamiliar audiences and at smaller venues than they would do at home.

This is certainly the case in the United States, and it's standard practice for an artist to split the representation of their live business – with an agent specifically focussed on North America, and another for the UK and everywhere else. This is partly due to visa considerations, and the requirement for a US promoter to provide necessary evidence of tour plans before a visa application can be completed. Having a reputed US agent onboard will undoubtedly streamline this process – although some superstar acts might bypass US agents completely and contract directly with a promoter.

Where an artist is working with two agents, those individuals won't necessarily work for the same agency (and, in fact, it's perfectly normal for them *not* to work for the same agency) but they will need to work in tandem when plotting and strategising touring plans. Some agents will also occasionally outsource to sub-agents in certain territories, for example in Asia where highly targeted local expertise might be required.

Aside from its size and scale and the range of opportunities on offer, there are some fundamental differences between North America's live music market and the rest of the world.

For a start, the US is far more consolidated. Although there are many independent promoters and venues, the market is dominated by the two global promoters: Live Nation and AEG Presents. These companies operate their own ticket companies (Ticketmaster and AXS) and have extensive control over networks of venues.

Consequently, and unlike the UK, where promoters tend to distribute tickets via multiple agents, in the US, inventory is typically allocated in its entirety to the single company that controls the venue box office. In other words, if your artist is playing a Live Nation building, then Ticketmaster will almost inevitably sell 100% of the tickets. Navigating such tightly controlled networks, and attempting to operate outside of them, is one area where the expertise of a US-based agent can be essential. There are also cultural differences in the US – for example with secondary ticketing, which, for some artists and promoters, is a far more accepted practice than it would be in the UK or Europe.

Similarly, while the US live business is dominated by the East and West coasts and venues around New York and Los Angeles, building an efficient touring schedule across the thousands of miles between other key cities – for example Nashville, Seattle, Atlanta, Philadelphia, Austin, Portland, Minneapolis or Chicago – will often require expert knowledge and local contacts.

Another key consideration will be choosing promoters for your shows. Similar to label or publisher negotiation, some managers will prefer to agree global partnerships with global corporations such as Live Nation or AEG Presents. Their size and scale can be advantageous, albeit their contracts will, reportedly, sometimes come with more restrictive exclusivity clauses that prevent artists from performing in certain locations or at certain events during specified time periods. (On the flip side, these promoters also operate a large portfolio of festivals, so working with them might also open additional opportunities to perform.) Depending on the size of the guarantee, they may also leverage a greater control of ticketing strategy – for instance, by utilising "dynamic" or "surge" pricing in order to increase yields.

For this reason, other managers will prefer to work with a combination of promoters or with independent operators. These might offer greater local expertise or expertise in a specific genre, as well as greater flexibility in terms of locations where tours are routed and how they are ticketed.

You will also want to ensure that your client is aware of any local customs or laws – and particularly in regards to alcohol or controlled substances. Why some US States, for instance, have legalised cannabis use, in other countries, possession can be a capital offence. With touring now an increasingly global business, with opportunities across Asia and the Middle East, such awareness becomes increasingly critical.

Touring at this scale will almost always require an expanded budget too. As an artist gains in popularity, they will usually increase spending on visuals, costume and stage production, supporting musicians, choreography and dancers, and an expanding crew. Tickets prices might go up, but so does the cost of the show. In addition to expenditure on accommodation, subsistence and transportation (instruments, equipment and production, as well as people), there will also be the possible per head costs of visas, expanding carnets and increasingly complex taxes and tarriffs to consider.

Certainly, any scale of international touring requires sound legal and financial counsel in advance – and potentially further expert advice from a visa specialist. In the US, for example, levels of withholding tax (taxes withheld by an overseas government on income received by non-residents) can be as high as 30% and vary state to state. To overcome this, managers often will consider appointing specific partners for overseas touring such as business managers, accountants or associates. Many UK based accountancy firms already have working partnerships or global offices in place.

As a result of the continuing uncertainties around Brexit, all covered in Part Two, this kind of advice is not isolated to North America – and, for the time being at least, you will undoubtedly require help from your accountant and lawyer to navigate European-based hurdles and the patchwork of new regulations resulting from the UK's decision to leave the EU.

Aside from speaking directly to MMF Associates with expertise in the live and touring sector, MMF members can also find a number of live-related resources through our website – including updated information on Brexit and US tour visas.

CHAPTER 11

Moving On. What Way To End It?

153
Mediation by Harry
Hodgkin & Dennis
Muirhead

Some artists and managers remain partners for life. However, music is a volatile business, and over the course of a career there are likely to be ups, downs, deviations and changes.

Many relationships will simply run their course. An artist might decide to stop making music, they might start a new project or collaboration, a band might split up, they might suffer health problems, or they might simply want different representation.

Some artists switch management companies on a regular basis.

All this can occur without acrimony, and, as explained in Part Two, this is the fundamental reason why most managers will want to agree a contract with their client in the first place - both to define the commercial boundaries of their relationship, and to ensure they can receive compensation and protection for their work via a sunset clause or post-commission agreement.

Inevitably, however, as with any relationship, there will be instances where an artist-manager partnership breaks down irretrievably. Notably, in one of the most high profile fall-outs of recent years, between Chance The Rapper and his manager Pat Corcoran, no written agreement was reportedly in place between the two parties. Their relationship was based purely on an oral understanding or handshake deal.

"There's an important lesson to learn that brings a great deal of freedom: nothing is forever but that doesn't mean it's not worth it. One thing you can count on as a manager is that you might get fired or separate with your talent. All management-artist relationships have a sell by date. But even if you're with them for 2 years it's okay. You need to realise that in what alternate universe do you expect to get a job for life? Managers should realise that if they work with 6 or 7 artists looking after each for a few years then that is a successful management career. You can still get sunset clauses, or you may have started a business with them or created something with them that you share in ownership. But you go on to the next one as there are always artists that will need your help, skills and experience. Success means doing something you love and moving on when the time is right."

Anneliese
Harmon
Music Exec,
Entrepreneur
and GM at
MMF

Similarly, there is increased scope for disagreement and disgruntlement when it comes to exercising a sunset clause – as well as a wider degree of contention as to what specific income these clauses should cover, and over what time period. As noted in the MMF's Managing Expectations report, some of this contention is being driven by changing dynamics within the industry, and the way in which streaming and social media have extended the life potential of recorded music.

Historically, a manager might have expected five years of full commission from a project they worked on, followed by five years on half commission – collecting a share of recorded and publishing revenue, as well as any brand-related income. (This is the basis for the example agreement agreed between the MMF, FAC and MU in 2021.) However, given current market complexities and the changing commercial dynamics between managers and artists, amicably resolving a separation agreement can be more challenging in practice.

For instance, some of the contentions that might arise, include:

- A manager may be apprehensive about inhibiting the development of an artist, and may seek to renegotiate the terms, especially if the immediate payment of post-term commission pushes them into debt.
- Communication breakdown. Without regular contact, or when an artist starts working with a new manager, or when dialogue takes place via lawyers, there can be increased potential for disagreement.

- Leverage and transparency. The artist will typically hold the power balance in a relationship, and the manager will be reliant on full disclosure of revenues and royalty statements.

- Timings. While some managers are happy to accept 5 or 10 year terms, others might consider longer agreements are more reflective of their efforts - particularly if they invested directly in an artist's projects.

- Global revenues. If the manager represented the artist in certain territories, or as part of a partnership, is it possible to extract which revenues are relevant to their agreement?

- Scope of revenues. With artists increasingly diversifying their business, what happens if they benefit from a new technology or partnership under the duration of the post-term agreement, or if this deal was brokered by a new manager?

Perhaps unsurprisingly, the 2019 research undertaken for our Managing Expectations report found that less than ⅔ of managers thought they had received less than they were due under their post-term agreement. This is a less than ideal situation, especially if the end goal here, as stated in the report is "*to reach an exit that does not foster growing animosities over the years.*"

If you are owed post-term commission according to your management contract and mediation has failed (see below) you may wish to take court action. If invoices remain ignored/unpaid after a reasonable period of notice then you can first send a 'letter before action' to the artist, copying their accountant serving notice that if the sum isn't paid by a set date you will go to the small claims court. There are sample letters before action you can find online and the small claims process up to £100,000 is accessible to all on payment of a fee which scales according to the amount owed. If you get no response or the defendant refuses to pay what they owe you can ask the court to order the defendant to pay. If the defendant says they do not owe you any money or they disagree with the amount you've claimed you may have to go to a hearing which could incur legal costs. However in many cases a letter before action is sufficient to spur payment.

MEDIATION BY HARRY HODGKIN & DENNIS MUIRHEAD

What is mediation?
Mediation is a way of resolving disputes without the need to go to court. If both parties in a dispute agree to mediation, then a trained mediator – who is always an impartial third party, skilled in the type of dispute that has arisen – guides the parties to a settlement on which they both agree. The mediator does not impose a decision or attempt to judge the merits of the case. The mediator's aim is to assist the parties equally and neutrally to a resolution.

Why is mediation not used in every case?

Where mediation might become difficult is getting both parties to agree that mediation is a good idea in the first place. Many disputes in the music industry inevitably become very personal, and the common-law legal system is geared to a combative approach: finding fault, picking holes, showing blame or error. People are all too often not inclined, by the very nature of the process, to settle, even when it is in their personal, career or commercial interests. They want their day in court. They want to show the other party that they were in the wrong. The only beneficiaries of this process are generally the parties' lawyers.

How does mediation overcome this?

Mediation looks at the common ground and the positive aspects then finds the best resolution for both parties. It identifies the risks both parties have in litigation and encourages them to assess the strengths and weaknesses of their case. It looks to the longer term and can explore the interests of the parties, both individually and together. Mediation can be (and is) used before or during the litigation process.

How does it work?

Mediation requires the consent of all parties, but if one or more have not indicated willingness, it's possible to approach a mediation provider so that they may help negotiate that initial agreement. The choice of mediator is important. It is generally best left to the mediation organisation to recommend a trained mediator with the relevant experience and, usually, knowledge of the subject. At an agreed time and venue, the mediator listens, allows the parties to express their feelings, explores underlying issues, challenging and encouraging where necessary.

The mediator spends time with each party, both in joint session and in private meetings, helping each party to focus on their interests and the interests of the other parties, rather than what they may perceive as their legal 'rights'. In commercial or contractual disputes, the mediator will explore the early part of the relationship, drawing out what it was that caused them to work together initially and what caused the breakdown in trust or confidence between the parties.

The mediator will help the parties to examine areas of possible agreement, as well as disagreement. Experience, skill and training are essential in this process. The mediator will also help each party to examine their own resolve, testing out their belief in the true strength of their own case and their resolve to fight rather than settle. Mediation is private, confidential and without prejudice.

Some of this process can be difficult, if not painful, for some parties, and for this reason the mediator will never test parties or try to expose weaknesses in a case in a joint session, only ever in private. All the discussions are completely confidential. The mediator will not repeat or imply to another party anything that one party has said unless or until the mediator has been given express permission to do so.

This confidentiality allows the parties to trust the mediator so that they can discuss openly all aspects of their case. Mediators and their providing organisations recognise the key importance of absolute confidentiality and discretion.

Details of mediations, arbitrations or settlements are never given by mediators. The parties may disclose them only if that is agreed within the terms of the settlement. This is an important facet of music industry mediation. Eventually, by spending time shuttling between the parties, the mediator can help the parties to understand their own and each other's positions in a way quite different to that of the traditional adversarial case and, in more than 80% of civil cases, reach an agreement on the day.

If no agreement is reached, the parties are not in any way bound by what has been discussed. The discussions are expressly without prejudice and may not be referred to in court. This confidentially is enshrined in a written mediation accord which the parties are required to sign before the mediation. If the parties settle the matter, the mediator will help them to draw up an agreement. This agreement becomes binding only once it has been drawn up and signed by the parties. If the agreement is not honoured, it may be enforced contractually or preferably by a further mediation.

Most agreements are honoured, though, precisely because the parties have worked hard to achieve a settlement and upon terms that were always within their control, unlike an imposed court decision.

Why mediate?
There are plenty of very good reasons, such as:

- The outcome of mediation is always within the control of the parties. With the help of the mediator, they decide for themselves upon a settlement they can live with.
- Parties in mediation avoid the uncertainty and dissatisfaction often experienced in court or at arbitration, where they have little choice but to accept the judgment, which may disappoint.
- Mediation resolves disputes fast, usually within a day, and can be arranged in days or weeks, and can last for as long as the parties want, ignoring conventional court hours.

- Mediation is very significantly less expensive than litigation, because months or years of litigation are avoided, as are the consequent fees of lawyers and experts. Parties may, of course (and generally do), have legal or other advisors present during the mediation if they wish.
- Mediation is voluntary – any party may withdraw at any time.
- There is strict confidentiality and neutrality.
- The parties often find that, at the end of the process, new common goals are established which sometimes allow for a full or partial reconciliation, or restoration of common production, songwriting, recording, performance or other aims.
- If the dispute ends up going to court, the parties are likely to be required to mediate (or to consider mediating) in any event, with costs consequences or delays if they fail to do so.

Court-based mediation

The advantages of mediation have become increasingly recognised by judges of the High Court and county courts. The present position is that the court is entitled to ask parties to provide evidence that they have considered using a dispute resolution process, the most commonly used process being mediation. Where a party is found to have unreasonably refused to mediate, the court is empowered to postpone the case until the required steps are taken or order the party at fault to pay adverse costs. At the time of writing the Ministry of Justice has issued proposals for introducing automatic referral to mediation for small claims (meaning at present most claims valued at up to £10,000) and, in due course, extending the requirement to mediate to all county court users.

Mediation is a key part of the civil court procedural reforms introduced by the former Lord Chief Justice Lord Woolf and the subsequent recommendations made by Lord Justice Jackson.

The Civil Mediation Council is a useful impartial contact and you can also search for a Civil Mediation Provider:

PPL offers alternative dispute resolution procedures to its members for disputes relating to the distribution of revenues collected by PPL for when a sound recording is played in public or broadcast in the UK. These processes aim to provide PPL members with a flexible, cost-effective, confidential and expeditious resolution for such disputes and includes adjudication, mediation and arbitration. More information can be found on the PPL website.

Harry Hodgkin is a practising barrister, arbitrator, accredited mediator and Head of Chambers at Clerksroom. He specialises in commercial and contractual disputes and property litigation.

Dennis Muirhead is an artist and record producer manager, and a business and legal affairs consultant. He is a mediator with The Association of Cambridge Mediators. He was a senior mediator with Clerksroom. Dennis was a co-founder of the law firm Simons Muirhead Burton in 1972 and a successful defence advocate particularly in drug cases. He was a co-founder and first chair of the MMF in 1992 and is now a custodian. Dennis was inducted into the MMF British Music Roll of Honour in 2008.

Conclusion
And That's a Wrap

This book has aimed to illustrate how changing music industry dynamics have elevated the role and the standing of the manager, and how managers are empowering artists, songwriters and music creators to navigate and plot a course through what is a highly fragmented commercial landscape.

This cottage industry of micro artist and creator-centric enterprises is increasingly the beating heart of what we define as "the music business". They are the ones creating value. The manager's role is to develop their creative and commercial activities, and to help build and expand their networks across a multiple of areas - whether that's live shows, recordings, publishing, brand partnerships, D2C activities or any other ancillary revenue streams.

Each manager will work with their client on a unique and individual journey.

There are no rules, only guidelines!

Supplementing these developments is the increased scope for artists to take greater ownership of their rights, and, in certain parts of the industry, to break free of historical conventions and deal structures. Again, the manager will play here, helping leverage the best possible partnerships for long-term global success.

This is all incredibly exciting and makes it the most fascinating and rewarding time to be involved in music management, with the potential to break new ground and to take artists into new and uncharted territories.

In this way, it also means the most established artists and music makers can effectively become a mini-industry in their own right – employing significant numbers of people as part of a core team, while indirectly providing work for many others. Again, managers are a catalyst for these changes, providing an inviolable link between the creative talent and the rest of the industry.

As well as future success for your own management business, we also hope you will engage closely with the MMF and input into our work - whether that's providing insights for groundbreaking research such as our *Dissecting The Digital Dollar*

Managing Expectations, or *Digital Burnout* reports, supporting upcoming managers through initiatives like the Accelerator Programme for Music Managers, participating in our training and educational work, or to helping us to advocate and develop policy.

Over recent years, MMF campaigns have led to significant changes across the business, from reforms in the streaming market and contractual terms to an overhaul of secondary ticketing.

In addition to being plugged into the boards of UK Music, LIVE and the Council of Music Makers, the MMF is increasingly active globally through the European Music Managers Alliance and partnerships with management representative bodies in the USA, Canada and Australia.

As a membership organisation, we are only as strong as the depth and diversity of our community and we would love you to become an active participant in everything that we do.

Join Us! www.theMMF.net

The Managers Backstage Toilet Wall: Secrets, Tips and Tricks

TOP 5 TIPS

Establish healthy boundaries with artists and collaborators!

Surround yourself with good people who have the same values.

Only manage people who work as hard or harder than you.

Sort paperwork early doors, even if it's terms over an email.

Trust your instinct and stop following the numbers

MMF Backstage Toilet Wall

EXPECTATION MANAGEMENT IS THE KEY TO EVERYTHING.

PATIENCE IS KEY. DON'T BE IN A HURRY TO GET IT WRONG.

An artist terminated our agreement out of the blue, claiming I'd abused their trust and taken advantage of their fragile mental health. Even though I (and all my colleagues) knew it was completely untrue, it left me questioning everything I'd done for the artist and knocked my confidence for months. I found out much later that they had done exactly the same thing to two previous managers and had regularly used it as a way to get out of contracts by threatening legal action against bullying. I guess my tip is 'stay true to yourself' and don't let manipulative personalities get in the way of doing what you know is right.

Advice that was given to me when I was feeling frustrated as the manager of an emerging band. "It's always too slow until it's too fast. Make the most of it by being too slow."

DON'T TAKE THINGS PERSONALLY.

LESS IS MORE, YOUR ARTISTS DO NOT NEED TO BE ACTIVE ON ALL SOCIAL MEDIA PLATFORMS. JUST FOCUS ON THE ONES THEY ENJOY BEING PART OF.

Always manage the whole person and their relationships, if you don't know what they're going through, you can't help them get ahead.

SOMETIMES WAITING IS BEST. OFTEN THINGS RESOLVE THEMSELVES.

DON'T BELIEVE THE HYPE AND STAY TRUE TO YOUR ART

MASTER VS SLAVE IS A MENTALITY. KNOW YOUR VALUE AND THE VALUE OF OWNERSHIP. THEY DON'T CALL THEM "MASTERS" FOR NOTHING.

Management should be collaborative and a partnership. Any artist that thinks you work for them, not with them, is likely to cause you undue stress and heartache!

I WISH THE INDUSTRY WOULD ADDRESS THE IMPORTANCE OF WORK-LIFE BALANCE. AS A YOUNG ENTREPRENEUR AND ARTIST MANAGER I FIND MYSELF HAVING TO BE TOLD TO REST AND NEGLECT MY FAMILY AND FRIENDS DURING BUSY TIMES.

OWNERSHIP = CONTROL + A LIVING

BE HONEST WITH YOURSELF - IF YOU KNOW YOU'RE NOT GOOD AT ONE THING, FIND SOMEONE ELSE WHO IS BETTER/THE BEST AND LEARN FROM THEM!

Never 'party' with a client at an after hours, a boundary needs to be set!

IF you won't have them as a houseguest, you can't effectively sell them as a pleasure to work with!

GET A THERAPIST IF YOU ARE STARTING TO BE OVERWHELMED, THIS INDUSTRY IS TRIGGER HEAVY.

THREE REASONS TO WORK WITH AN ARTIST: YOU LOVE THE MUSIC, YOU'RE PASSIONATE ABOUT THE ARTIST OR THE MONEY IS GOOD. MEATLOAF GOT IT RIGHT — TWO OUT OF THREE AIN'T BAD.

"Date" artists/labels/ publishers before signing a deal. Making sure they walk the walk not just talk the talk.

The number one rule... Your clients are NOT your friends!

DON'T BE AFRAID OF MISTAKES — THEY ONLY MAKE YOU BETTER!

PATIENCE IS KEY. DON'T BE IN A HURRY TO GET IT WRONG.

STAY PATIENT AND STAY POSITIVE, YOU CAN ACHIEVE EVERYTHING YOU WANT BUT IT TAKES TIME

ALWAYS SLEEP ON IT BEFORE REACTING ESPECIALLY WHEN YOU ARE ANGRY OR FRUSTRATED.

Never tell publishing A&R that covers aren't a priority.

BUILD GREAT TEAMS BUT DON'T RELY ON THEM, MAKE SURE YOU KNOW WHAT YOUR AIMS FOR YOUR CLIENT IS AND DON'T LET SOMEONE ELSE'S AIMS TAKE OVER.

PARTNERSHIP NOT OWNERSHIP

MMF Backstage Toilet Wall

MAKE
MORE
MISTAKES

If you won't have them as a houseguest, you can't effectively sell them as a pleasure to work with!

SOMETIMES WAITING IS BEST. OFTEN THINGS RESOLVE THEMSELVES.

IF you're taking 20% of their income, they should get 20% of your time – effective time management as a manager will help prevent burnout. Will ebb and flow but as an average.

DON'T TAKE THINGS PERSONALLY.

DON'T SHARE IDEAS OR SUCCESSES TILL THE INK IS DRY

Master vs Slave is a mentality. Know your value and the value of ownership. They don't call them "Masters" for nothing.

Don't be afraid of mistakes - they only make you better! The most successful people I know in the industry have made the most mistakes. Just don't make the same mistake twice.

Expectation management is the key to everything.

DON'T BELIEVE THE HYPE AND STAY TRUE TO YOUR ART

THE "TRUTH" OF THE MANAGEMENT BUSINESS WILL SET YOU FREE...BUT FIRST IT WILL PISS YOU OFF. SEEK IT ANYWAY

I WISH THE INDUSTRY THOUGHT MORE CONSCIOUSLY ABOUT WHO WE CHOSE TO PLATFORM FROM BOTH AN ARTIST STAND POINT AND FROM INDUSTRY PROFESSIONALS. BEING SUCCESSFUL DOESN'T AUTOMATICALLY MAKE A PERSON A GOOD ROLE MODEL OR MEAN THEY HAVE A POSITIVE IMPACT ON THE WORLD. WE HAVE DAILY OPPORTUNITIES TO PRIORITISE THESE THINGS WHILE CREATING SUCCESS AND SUSTAINED CAREERS IN MUSIC.

The mainstream industry wasn't looking for The Beatles, or Hendrix, or The Smiths, or punk, or metal, or hip hop, or rave so if you're doing something you believe in KEEP DOING IT!

If you won't have them as a houseguest, you can't effectively sell them as a pleasure to work with!

Remember who you work for!

Only sit at tables where respect is being served.

NEVER TELL PUBLISHING A&R THAT COVERS AREN'T A PRIORITY.

"NEVER 'PARTY' WITH A CLIENT AT AN AFTER HOURS, A BOUNDARY NEEDS TO BE SET!

I WOULD LOVE ARTIST'S MANAGERS TO BE A LOT BETTER EDUCATED ABOUT THE ROLE OF THE PRODUCER / SONGWRITER AND VALUE THEIR INPUT WAY MORE IN TERMS OF GENEROSITY, ON BADLY PAID OR TIGHT BUDGET PROJECTS. PRODUCERS AND SONGWRITERS CONTINUE TO GET THE CRAPPIEST SHARE OF A PROJECT – DESPITE OFTEN WORKING FOR FREE – THIS REALLY NEEDS TO CHANGE.

THE NUMBER ONE RULE...YOUR CLIENTS ARE NOT YOUR FRIENDS!

You can never know it all, yet as long as we are open to each other's energy we will all be the mightier

LIFE'S TOO SHORT TO WORK WITH ****HOLES

SIGN THE SHORTEST LONG-TERM RECORD DEAL AS YOU CAN (1 TO 3 ALBUMS). YOU WANT THE LABEL THINKING, INVESTING, BUILDING AND FIGHTING FOR THE LONG TERM (NOT JUST FOR ONE EP) BUT ALSO NEED A POINT TO RE-NEGOTIATE OR EXTEND THE DEAL OR AN EXIT STRATEGY.

MANAGE YOUR BUSINESS AS WELL AS YOUR ARTISTS

Write down your own tips and tricks...

MMF Jargon Buster

The Music Business loves its acronyms! You may see a few in this book and you'll certainly come across more in your management career. Here's our starter guide to the jargon (alternatively a glossary of music industry terms). Let us know if we're missing any and we'll include them in a future edition.

A1 – a form that proves your artist/crew is paying social security contributions in the UK and so does not also have to pay these in the other countries they are performing in

AIF – Association of Independent Festivals

AIM – Association of Independent Music, representing the rights holders of non-major recorded rights. Their members are indie labels, distributors and artists who own their own rights.

ASCAP – American Society of Composers Authors and Publishers a US Performing Rights Collecting Society for song royalties

BMI – Broadcast Music Inc a US Performing Rights Collecting Society for song royalties

BPI – British Phonographic Industry (major & independent record labels). They also have a whole team focused on tackling digital piracy as well as lobbying the government. As well as the 3 majors they also represent a number of indie labels.

BRIT Awards – annual awards show run by the BPI, raises funding for the Brit Trust which supports the Brit School in Croydon and other music charities

Carnet – a kind of passport for your equipment (goods rather than people) which proves you are taking back what you took out and so do not have to pay import taxes

CISAC – the International Confederation of Societies of Authors and Composers

CMO – Collective Management Organisation

CMU – Complete Music Update (daily music biz newsletter plus training courses)

CRB – Copyright Royalty Board a regulatory authority that sets song royalty rates in the US only

D2F – Direct to Fan

DCMS – UK Government Department for Culture Media and Sport

DIT – UK Government Department for International Trade

DSP – Digital Service Provider e.g. a streaming service such as Spotify, Apple Music, YouTube Music or Amazon Music.

EMMA – European Music Managers Alliance. MMF UK is a member of EMMA to connect us with other management organisations and share knowledge.

FAC – Featured Artists Coalition (e.g. represents signed or independent artists)

Force Majeure- is an event that happens outside of your control, including natural disasters, civil unrest, 'acts of God' and any other unforeseeable event that could disrupt your trip.

Help Musicians – previously known as the UK Benevolent Fund provides crisis funding, development funding and touring support as well as running Music Minds Matter and the Bullying and Harassment helpline.

IFPI – International Federation of the Phonographic Industry (label's international lobby group

ISM – Incorporated Society of Musicians

Ivors Academy – previously BASCA – represents songwriters and composers and runs the prestigious Ivor Novello awards

LIVE – Association of Live Music in the UK, MMF is a Board member

MCPS – Mechanical Copyright Protection Society

MDRC – Minimum Delivery Release Commitments

MEGS – Music Export Growth Scheme, money for overseas touring and promotion, administered by the BPI with funding provided by the Government's Department for International Trade

MFN- Most Favoured Nation, legal term where two or more parties will be entitled to the same or better

MMF – Music Managers Forum

MPA – Music Publishers Association

MPG – Music Producers Guild

MU – Musicians Union

NFT – Non-fungible Token

NMPA – National Music Publishers Association (US)

Perpetuity – for the lifetime of the copyright e.g. 70 years from date of recording or 70 years from the death of the author (e.g. a very long time)

Point – percentage point which determines the royalty rate e.g. 4 points to the producer is 4 percentage points out of the artist's royalty (if this is 22% then that leaves the artist with 18%). Even with streaming this is often still based on the notional PPD rate (see below).

PPD – Published Price to Dealer

PPL – Phonographic Performance Limited

PRO – Performance Rights Organisation administering song royalties e.g. PRS/BMI/ASCAP

PRS – Performing Rights Society – the UK PRO

PRSF – The PRS Foundation is a charity funded by PRS, PPL and a host of other supporters, it runs the Momentum grant, International Showcase fund and a host of other grants for music makers

SESAC – The Society of European Stage Authors and Composers the second-oldest performance-rights organization in the United States collecting song royalties.

Split – the division of ownership of a song or recording e.g. if there are 4 contributors to a track they could split the publishing 25/25/25/25 or may split it dependent of value of contribution e.g. 40% to the main songwriter, 20 each to the other contributors.

SXSW – South By South West – the world's biggest music showcase festival in Austin, Texas with big international presence each March

TGE – The Great Escape – the UK's biggest music showcase festival in Brighton each May

UMG – Universal Music Group

Withholding Tax – a tax deducted at source, especially one levied by some countries on interest or dividends paid to a person resident outside that country

WMG – Warner Music Group

Printed in Great Britain
by Amazon